Economic Justice:

CTU's Pastoral Commentary on the Bishops' Letter on the Economy

John Pawlikowski and
Donald Senior,

editors

The Pastoral Press
Washington, D.C.

ISBN 0-912405-41-4

© 1988 by The Pastoral Press

The Pastoral Press
225 Sheridan Street, NW
Washington, DC 20011
(202) 723-1254

The Pastoral Press is the publications division of the National Association of Pastoral Musicians, a membership organization of musicians and clergy dedicated to fostering the art of musical liturgy.

Printed in the United States of America

Contents

Editors' Preface

Twice in this decade, the Catholic bishops of the United States have confronted moral issues which reach deep into American society, culture, and politics. In *The Challenge of Peace* (1983) the bishops urged a reversal of the nuclear arms race and the construction of a new international order for development and peace. Three years later, in *Economic Justice for All*, they argued that deep-going reforms in the U.S. economic structure are necessary. Neither document offered hard-and-fast specific solutions. Both are intended to bring about a wide-spread discussion within the church and beyond it—a moral re-examination of our nation's purpose and policies. What effect the pastoral letters will have, depends much on people like the readers of this book, who are willing to ponder the implications of their Christian faith.

This commentary carries forward a dialogue which began before the bishops' drafting committee wrote a word of the letter on the American economy. The committee members listened first—to business people and labor leaders, to economists and government officials, to theologians and community workers and farmers and poor people. At each stage of the letter's development, critical response was asked and received; thousands of Catholics and others had an impact on the final document.

The reader of this book will find at the end of each chapter questions for discussion. These are not extras tacked on. For this volume aims not only to respond to highlights of the bishops' letter, but also to provoke personal reflection and a more informed ethical discussion among Catholics and other citizens. It raises questions such as, what is really at stake in daily work and spending, in our government's economic policies, or in the various proposals for creating jobs or changing the ground rules of the global economic order?

At the beginning of the book the reader will find the bishops' Pastoral Message which introduces the pastoral. This Message sets forth the principle themes of the pastoral and is reproduced for the convenience of the reader.

In *Economic Justice for All* a vision of the kind of life to which God calls us today is developed. It is a vision summoned up from the Bible and Catholic tradition. It is given distinctive coloring by hope—the yearning for a world which is shaped by everyone's free decisions, supports everyone's dignity and rights, and expresses the solidarity of all members of God's human family. The vision is translated into a common moral language of values, principles, rights, and responsibilities, so that Catholics can better take part in public discussion about the direction in which the American economy should move. Key economic challenges—persistent poverty, creation of worthwhile jobs, erosion of family farming, and arrested development in the poor countries—are addressed. The bishops also call for greater democracy in the way economic decisions are made.

But the pastoral letter returns finally to what all of this means for deeper conversion to Christ, for faithful discipleship, the practice of Christian communities, and the American Catholic Church's justice-making mission in the world. Accordingly, the majority of essays that follow develop elements of a Christian vision of economic activity, while the concluding pieces deal with communicating the message in Catholic communities. The authors do not pretend to cover all the bases of the pastoral, but rather chart major themes and reflect on the material in the pastoral from many complementary angles. They invite you the reader to question and build on their perspectives, on the basis of your own faith, experience, and knowledge. Thus you will be carrying on the dialogue of conscience which the bishops wanted to provoke. If a large number of Catholics in this country engage in such critical, collaborative dialogue, a crucial step will have been taken towards creating "economic justice for all."

The contributors to this volume are members of the faculty of Catholic Theological Union, a graduate school of ministry in Chicago. Because they represent a wide range of theological vantage points, they are an apt group to comment on a pastoral letter which is itself a consensus document incorporating diverse theological elements. The authors also bring to their task the experience of interacting with all sorts of students, young and old, men and women, laypeople and religious, U.S. and foreign citizens; in short, their perspectives have been influenced by people from many different backgrounds and circumstances of life. Finally, many of the contributors have spent time in the poor countries of the Third World, and thus have a sharp awareness of the effects of a global economy whose basic structure and workings have been heavily determined by the United States.

The chapters of this book fall into three major subdivisions.

The Biblical Perspective. Four essays lay down biblical foundations for a theology of economic activity. Dianne Bergant, C.S.A., Associate Professor of Old Testament, shows how human dignity is rooted in our being created in the image and likeness of God. The opening chapters of Genesis also reveal a communal relationship with the earth. God alone is sovereign. The control which we exercise over the earth must be in accord with the life processes of our fellow living creatures; any economic order must respect the right of all people to live from the earth's riches and to participate in stewardship of its resources. Leslie Hoppe, O.F.M., Associate Professor of Old Testament, finds a complementary notion of biblical justice in the book of Deuteronomy. The land's bounty is given by God to all and belongs to no one absolutely. The people of Israel belong to one family, and so are not to be permanently divided into an economically powerful class and an economically dependent class. Moreover, that people's relationship with God was a product of the societal relationships existing among themselves.

Carroll Stuhlmueller, C.P., Professor of Old Testament, traces how "the poor" are at the center of the Hebrew prophets' and Jesus' demand for faithfulness to God's covenant. Salvation or ruin depend on how we respond to the affliction and outcry of the poor. An abundant land will be retained on loan from God only if we actively try to achieve the prophetic dream of bread and work for all. Turning to the New Testament, Donald Senior, C.P., Professor of New Testament, brings out the central Gospel call to discipleship. Following Jesus means absorbing and embodying, in our own social and economic circumstances, the values of God's Reign—that is, Jesus' inclusive, compassionate, and just vision of the human family.

2 *The Ethical Perspective.* Four essays examine themes or key concepts of recent Catholic social teaching. Those theme and concepts help us to move from a vision of economic life into the practical work of, first, building greater justice into what the U.S. economy does for people and to people; and second, enabling more people to take charge of their own economic advancement and share responsibility for the nation's future (cf. the *Pastoral*, #1). John Pawlikowski, O.S.M., Professor of Social Ethics, exposes one of the best-kept secrets of American Catholicism. For a century Catholics have strongly influenced the American labor movement. Out of that activism arose a series of episcopal statements on economic issues—often prophetic and sometimes politically effective—which laid the groundwork for *Economic Justice for All*. Thomas Nairn, O.F.M., Assistant Professor of Ethics, reaches back to the "common moral vision" found in the Catholic Church down through the centuries. Recent papal social documents expanded this traditional vision to embrace a global church and a world economic order. The realities of human dignity and an interdependent economic order, seen in contrast to the reality of massive poverty, constitute for us an urgent call to a deeper conversion made effective in action.

Two further essays offer different readings of economic ethics. Paul Wadell, C.P., Assistant Professor of Ethics, finds the common good to be the bishops' central theme; and commitment to it, that which makes possible a just economy. He sees conversion as needed if we are to become committed to the common good. In a Christian reading of the world, the nature of the common good is recognized only in light of God. Doing justice requires transforming ourselves accordingly and means re-forming our society to be more like God's Kingdom. For John Paul Szura, O.S.A., Associate Professor of Psychology and Theology, two realities—persons' economic rights and their needing one another's support to develop fully—are at the heart of the pastoral letter's vision. In recent Catholic social teaching, the "principle of subsidiarity" relates these two realities. Subsidiarity means that personal dignity is fulfilled and rights insured by "helping communities" of various kinds. In economics, the principle challenges us to find ways to invite outsiders into the banquet of life.

The Pastoral Perspective. The remaining four essays set out some implications of the document for pastoral ministry. All touch on repentance and conversion. The importance of this section is underlined by the fact that the National Conference of Catholic Bishops decided to commit more resources to follow-up on this pastoral letter than it did in the case of the Peace Pastoral, which slipped into limbo in all too many dioceses and parishes. In many respects, the vision of economic life which the bishops have set forth is strongly counter-cultural. The message will be heard and acted on only if pastoral ministers make a determined, long-term effort to evangelize the church and evangelize American culture, to use terms in which Pope Paul VI spoke about evangelization.

Marie McCarthy, S.P., Assistant Professor of Pastoral Care, explores the spiritual and psychological dynamics involved in the journey of conversion toward a just society. Love, justice, and mutuality are the desired foundations, but psychic impediments to them have to be overcome. The journey is possible only if undertaken within a caring community. Liturgy, which lies at the heart of a Christian community, fundamentally expresses its mission to justice, writes Edward Foley, a Capuchin and Assistant Professor of Liturgy. Liturgy is both an expression of and impetus for justice, and is in itself a just act. The eucharist he sees as a special "rehearsal" of our mission in justice.

For religious educators and parents, a methodology and practical suggestions are offered by Jeanette Lucinio, S.P., Instructor in Religious Education. She shows how values and concepts from the pastoral can be integrated into students' experience and wider learning, not superimposed from outside. Given the letter's content, a method of critical reflection is appropriate: reflected-upon experience is brought into interaction with the Christian story. Overall, says Fred Hang, C.S.S.R., Instructor in Preaching and Communications, it is a question of *communicating* the pastoral letter. In his suggestions for effective communication, he follows the bishops' lead in urging that people's experiences and insights be respected, and special attention be paid to the point of view of poor and powerless people.

The editors wish to dedicate this commentary to Archbishop Rembert Weakland, O.S.B. of Milwaukee and the episcopal committee whose inspired leadership made possible this very important pastoral letter on the economy. Gratitude is likewise due to Fr. Francis J. Schuele of the Diocese of Kansas City, Missouri, for valuable editorial work on this volume.

John T. Pawlikowski, O.S.M.
Donald Senior, C.P.

A Pastoral Message
ECONOMIC JUSTICE FOR ALL

Brothers and Sisters in Christ:

1. We are believers called to follow Our Lord Jesus Christ and proclaim his Gospel in the midst of a complex and powerful economy. This reality poses both opportunities and responsibilities for Catholics in the United States. Our faith calls us to measure this economy, not only by what it produces, but also by how it touches human life and whether it protects or undermines the dignity of the human person. Economic decisions have human consequences and moral content; they help or hurt people, strengthen or weaken family life, advance or diminish the quality of justice in our land.

2. This is why we have written *Economic Justice for All: A Pastoral Letter on Catholic Social Teaching and the U.S. Economy.* This letter is a personal invitation to Catholics to use the resources of our faith, the strength of our economy, and the opportunities of our democracy to shape a society that better protects the dignity and basic rights of our sisters and brothers, both in this land and around the world.

3. The pastoral letter has been a work of careful inquiry, wide consultation, and prayerful discernment. The letter has been greatly enriched by this process of listening and refinement. We offer this introductory pastoral message to Catholics

in the United States seeking to live their faith in the market-place—in homes, offices, factories, and schools; on farms and ranches; in boardrooms and union halls; in service agencies and legislative chambers. We seek to explain why we wrote the pastoral letter, to introduce its major themes, and to share our hopes for the dialogue and action it might generate.

Why We Write

4. We write to share our teaching, to raise questions, to challenge one another to live our faith in the world. We write as heirs of the biblical prophets who summon us "to do the right, and to love goodness, and to walk humbly with your God" (Mi 6:8). We write as followers of Jesus who told us in the Sermon on the Mount: "Blessed are the poor in spirit . . . Blessed are the meek . . . Blessed are they who hunger and thirst for righteousness . . . You are the salt of the earth . . . You are the light of the world" (Mt 5:1-6, 13-14). These words challenge us not only as believers but also as consumers, citizens, workers, and owners. In the parable of the Last Judgment, Jesus said, "For I was hungry and you gave me food, I was thirsty and you gave me drink . . . As often as you did it for one of my least brothers, you did it for me" (Mt 25:35-40). The challenge for us is to discover in our own place and time what it means to be "poor in spirit" and "the salt of the earth" and what it means to serve "the least among us" and to "hunger and thirst for righteousness."

5. Followers of Christ must avoid a tragic separation between faith and everyday life. They can neither shirk their earthly duties nor, as the Second Vatican Council declared, "immerse [them]selves in earthly activities as if these latter were utterly foreign to religion, and religion were nothing more than the fulfillment of acts of worship and the observance of a few moral obligations" (*Pastoral Constitution on the Church in the Modern World*, no. 43).

6. Economic life raises important social and moral questions for each of us and for society as a whole. Like family life, economic life is one of the chief areas where we live out our faith, love our neighbor, confront temptation, fulfill God's

creative design, and achieve our holiness. Our economic activity in factory, field, office, or shop feeds our families—or feeds our anxieties. It exercises our talents—or wastes them. It raises our hopes—or crushes them. It brings us into cooperation with others—or sets us at odds. The Second Vatican Council instructs us "to preach the message of Christ in such a way that the light of the Gospel will shine on all activities of the faithful" (*Pastoral Constitution*, no. 43). In this case, we are trying to look at economic life through the eyes of faith, applying traditional church teaching to the U.S. economy.

7. In our letter, we write as pastors, not public officials. We speak as moral teachers, not economic technicians. We seek not to make some political or ideological point but to lift up the human and ethical dimensions of economic life, aspects too often neglected in public discussion. We bring to this task a dual heritage of Catholic social teaching and traditional American values.

8. As *Catholics*, we are heirs of a long tradition of thought and action on the moral dimensions of economic activity. The life and words of Jesus and the teaching of his Church call us to serve those in need and to work actively for social and economic justice. As a community of believers, we know that our faith is tested by the quality of justice among us, that we can best measure our life together by how the poor and the vulnerable are treated. This is not a new concern for us. It is as old as the Hebrew prophets, as compelling as the Sermon on the Mount, and as current as the powerful voice of Pope John Paul II defending the dignity of the human person.

9. As *Americans*, we are grateful for the gift of freedom and committed to the dream of "liberty and justice for all." This nation, blessed with extraordinary resources, has provided an unprecedented standard of living for millions of people. We are proud of the strength, productivity, and creativity of our economy, but we also remember those who have been left behind in our progress. We believe that we honor our history best by working for the day when all our sisters and brothers share adequately in the American dream.

10. As bishops, in proclaiming the Gospel for these times we also manage institutions, balance budgets, meet payrolls. In this we see the human face of our economy. We feel the

hurts and hopes of our people. We feel the pain of our sisters and brothers who are poor, unemployed, homeless, living on the edge. The poor and vulnerable are on our doorsteps, in our parishes, in our service agencies, and in our shelters. We see too much hunger and injustice, too much suffering and despair, both in our own country and around the world.

11. As pastors, we also see the decency, generosity, and vulnerability of our people. We see the struggles of ordinary families to make ends meet and to provide a better future for their children. We know the desire of managers, professionals, and business people to shape what they do by what they believe. It is the faith, good will, and generosity of our people that gives us hope as we write this letter.

Principal Themes of the Pastoral Letter

12. The pastoral letter is not a blueprint for the American economy. It does not embrace any particular theory of how the economy works, nor does it attempt to resolve the disputes between different schools of economic thought. Instead, our letter turns to Scripture and to the social teachings of the Church. There, we discover what our economic life must serve, what standards it must meet. Let us examine some of these basic moral principles.

13. *Every economic decision and institution must be judged in light of whether it protects or undermines the dignity of the human person.* The pastoral letter begins with the human person. We believe the person is sacred—the clearest reflection of God among us. Human dignity comes from God, not from nationality, race, sex, economic status, or any human accomplishment. We judge any economic system by what it does *for* and *to* people and by how it permits all to *participate* in it. The economy should serve people, not the other way around.

14. *Human dignity can be realized and protected only in community.* In our teaching, the human person is not only sacred but also social. How we organize our society—in economics and politics, in law and policy—directly affects human dignity and the capacity of individuals to grow in community. The obligation to "love our neighbor" has an individual dimen-

sion, but it also requires a broader social commitment to the common good. We have many partial ways to measure and debate the health of our economy: Gross National Product, per capita income, stock market prices, and so forth. The Christian vision of economic life looks beyond them all and asks, Does economic life enhance or threaten our life together as a community?

15. *All people have a right to participate in the economic life of society.* Basic justice demands that people be assured a minimum level of participation in the economy. It is wrong for a person or group to be excluded unfairly or to be unable to participate or contribute to the economy. For example, people who are both able and willing, but cannot get a job are deprived of the participation that is so vital to human development. For, it is through employment that most individuals and families meet their material needs, exercise their talents, and have an opportunity to contribute to the larger community. Such participation has a special significance in our tradition because we believe that it is a means by which we join in carrying forward God's creative activity.

16. *All members of society have a special obligation to the poor and vulnerable.* From the Scriptures and church teaching, we learn that the justice of a society is tested by the treatment of the poor. The justice that was the sign of God's covenant with Israel was measured by how the poor and unprotected—the widow, the orphan, and the stranger—were treated. The kingdom that Jesus proclaimed in his word and ministry excludes no one. Throughout Israel's history and in early Christianity, the poor are agents of God's transforming power. "The Spirit of the Lord is upon me, therefore he has anointed me. He has sent me to bring glad tidings to the poor" (Lk 4:18). This was Jesus' first public utterance. Jesus takes the side of those most in need. In the Last Judgment, so dramatically described in St. Matthew's Gospel, we are told that we will be judged according to how we respond to the hungry, the thirsty, the naked, the stranger. As followers of Christ, we are challenged to make a fundamental "option for the poor"—to speak for the voiceless, to defend the defenseless, to assess life styles, policies, and social institutions in terms of their impact on the poor. This "option for the poor" does not mean pitting one

group against another, but rather, strengthening the whole community by assisting those who are most vulnerable. As Christians, we are called to respond to the needs of *all* our brothers and sisters, but those with the greatest needs require the greatest response.

17. *Human rights are the minimum conditions for life in community.* In Catholic teaching, human rights include not only civil and political rights but also economic rights. As Pope John XXIII declared, "all people have a right to life, food, clothing, shelter, rest, medical care, education, and employment." This means that when people are without a chance to earn a living, and must go hungry and homeless, they are being denied basic rights. Society must ensure that these rights are protected. In this way, we will ensure that the minimum conditions of economic justice are met for all our sisters and brothers.

18. *Society as a whole, acting through public and private institutions, has the moral responsibility to enhance human dignity and protect human rights.* In addition to the clear responsibility of private institutions, government has an essential responsibility in this area. This does not mean that government has the primary or exclusive role, but it does have a positive moral responsibility in safeguarding human rights and ensuring that the minimum conditions of human dignity are met for all. In a democracy, government is a means by which we can act together to protect what is important to us and to promote our common values.

19. These six moral principles are not the only ones presented in the pastoral letter, but they given an overview of the moral vision that we are trying to share. This vision of economic life cannot exist in a vacuum; it must be translated into concrete measures. Our pastoral letter spells out some specific applications of Catholic moral principles. We call for a new national commitment to full employment. We say it is a social and moral scandal that one of every seven Americans is poor, and we call for concerted efforts to eradicate poverty. The fulfillment of the basic needs of the poor is of the highest priority. We urge that all economic policies be evaluated in light of their impact on the life and stability of the family. We support measures to halt the loss of family farms and to resist

the growing concentration in the ownership of agricultural resources. We specify ways in which the United States can do far more to relieve the plight of poor nations and assist in their development. We also reaffirm church teaching on the rights of workers, collective bargaining, private property, subsidiarity, and equal opportunity.

20. We believe that the recommendations in our letter are reasonable and balanced. In analyzing the economy, we reject ideological extremes and start from the fact that ours is a "mixed" economy, the product of a long history of reform and adjustment. We know that some of our specific recommendations are controversial. As bishops, we do not claim to make these prudential judgments with the same kind of authority that marks our declarations of principle. But, we feel obliged to teach by example how Christians can undertake concrete analysis and make specific judgments on economic issues. The Church's teachings cannot be left at the level of appealing generalities.

21. In the pastoral letter, we suggest that the time has come for a "New American Experiment"—to implement economic rights, to broaden the sharing of economic power, and to make economic decisions more accountable to the common good. This experiment can create new structures of economic partnership and participation within firms at the regional level, for the whole nation, and across borders.

22. Of course, there are many aspects of the economy the letter does not touch, and there are basic questions it leaves to further exploration. There are also many specific points on which men and women of good will may disagree. We look for a fruitful exchange among differing viewpoints. We pray only that all will take to heart the urgency of our concerns; that together we will test our views by the Gospel and the Church's teaching; and that we will listen to other voices in a spirit of mutual respect and open dialogue.

A Call to Conversion and Action

23. We should not be surprised if we find Catholic social teaching to be demanding. The Gospel is demanding. We are

always in need of conversion, of a change of heart. We are richly blessed, and as St. Paul assures us, we are destined for glory. Yet, it is also true that we are sinners; that we are not always wise or loving or just; that, for all our amazing possibilities, we are incompletely born, wary of life, and hemmed in by fears and empty routines. We are unable to entrust ourselves fully to the living God, and so we seek substitute forms of security in material things, in power, in indifference, in popularity, in pleasure. The Scriptures warn us that these things can become forms of idolatry. We know that, at times, in order to remain truly a community of Jesus' disciples, we will have to say "no" to certain aspects in our culture, to certain trends and ways of acting that are opposed to a life of faith, love and justice. Changes in our hearts lead naturally to a desire to change how we act. With what care, human kindness, and justice do I conduct myself at work? How will my economic decisions to buy, sell, invest, divest, hire, or fire serve human dignity and the common good? In what career can I best exercise my talents so as to fill the world with the Spirit of Christ? How do my economic choices contribute to the strength of my family and community, to the values of my children, to a sensitivity to those in need? In this consumer society, how can I develop a healthy detachment from things and avoid the temptation to assess who I am by what I have? How do I strike a balance between labor and leisure that enlarges my capacity for friendships, for family life, for community? What government policies should I support to attain the well-being of all, especially the poor and vulnerable?

24. The answers to such questions are not always clear— or easy to live out. But, conversion is a lifelong process. And, it is not undertaken alone. It occurs with the support of the whole believing community, through baptism, common prayer, and our daily efforts, large and small, on behalf of justice. As a Church, we must be people after God's own heart, bonded by the Spirit, sustaining one another in love, setting our hearts on God's kingdom, committing ourselves to solidarity with those who suffer, working for peace and justice, acting as a sign of Christ's love and justice in the world. The Church cannot redeem the world from the deadening effects of sin and injustice unless it is working to remove sin and

injustice in its own life and institutions. All of us must help the Church to practice in its own life what it preaches to others about economic justice and cooperation.

25. The challenge of this pastoral letter is not merely to think differently, but also to act differently. A renewal of economic life depends on the conscious choices and commitments of individual believers who practice their faith in the world. The road to holiness for most of us lies in our secular vocations. We need a spirituality that calls forth and supports lay initiative and witness not just in our churches but also in business, in the labor movement, in the professions, in education, and in public life. Our faith is not just a weekend obligation, a mystery to be celebrated around the altar on Sunday. It is a pervasive reality to be practiced every day in homes, offices, factories, schools, and businesses across our land. We cannot separate what we believe from how we act in the marketplace and the broader community, for this is where we make our primary contribution to the pursuit of economic justice.

26. We ask each of you to read the pastoral letter, to study it, to pray about it, and match it with your own experience. We ask you to join with us in service to those in need. Let us reach out personally to the hungry and the homeless, to the poor and the powerless, and to the troubled and the vulnerable. In serving them, we serve Christ. Our service efforts cannot substitute for just and compassionate public policies, but they can help us practice what we preach about human life and human dignity.

27. The pursuit of economic justice takes believers into the public arena, testing the policies of government by the principles of our teaching. We ask you to become more informed and active citizens, using your voices and votes to speak for the voiceless, to defend the poor and the vulnerable and to advance the common good. We are called to shape a constituency of conscience, measuring every policy by how it touches the least, the lost, and the left-out among us. This letter calls us to conversion and common action, to new forms of stewardship, service, and citizenship.

28. The completion of a letter such as this is but the beginning of a long process of education, discussion, and action. By faith and baptism, we are fashioned into new creatures,

filled with the Holy Spirit and with a love that compels us to seek out a new profound relationship with God, with the human family, and with all created things. Jesus has entered our history as God's anointed son who announces the coming of God's kingdom, a kingdom of justice and peace and freedom. And, what Jesus proclaims, he embodies in his actions. His ministry reveals that the reign of God is something more powerful than evil, injustice, and the hardness of hearts. Through his crucifixion and resurrection, he reveals that God's love is ultimately victorious over all suffering, all horror, all meaninglessness, and even over the mystery of death. Thus, we proclaim words of hope and assurance to all who suffer and are in need.

29. We believe that the Christian view of life, including economic life, can transform the lives of individuals, families, schools, and our whole culture. We believe that with your prayers, reflection, service, and action, our economy can be shaped so that human dignity prospers and the human person is served. This is the unfinished work of our nation. This is the challenge of our faith.

Economic Justice:

CTU's Pastoral
Commentary on
the Bishops' Letter
on the Economy

THE BIBLICAL
PERSPECTIVE

1

Stewards of the Household
of God

Dianne Bergant, C.S.A.

"THE BASIS FOR ALL THAT THE CHURCH BELIEVES ABOUT THE MORAL
dimensions of economic life is its vision of the transcendent
worth—the sacredness—of human beings" (#28). This statement expresses the principal theme of the American bishops'
pastoral letter *Economic Justice for All*. Throughout the letter they
insist that people, not goods, must be the primary concern of a
healthy and just economic system. This conviction is based on
a long tradition of Catholic social thought and is rooted in the
Bible.

While the sacred Scriptures do not provide us with specific
answers to the pressing complex economic questions of our day,
they do offer us a religious point of view from which to address
these questions. It is there that we discover the faith of our
ancestors, both Israelite and Christian. It is from there that the
bishops derive the character of their moral vision. "The focal
points of Israel's faith—creation, covenant and community—
provide a foundation for reflections on issues of economic and
social justice" (#30).

3

CREATED IN GOD'S IMAGE

The Dignity That Is Ours

"Human dignity comes from God" (Pastoral Message #13). The bishops are very clear about this. It is not something bestowed on us by another because of some accomplishment we may have achieved or some possession we may have acquired. It is ours in virtue of our being created by God. We are the handiwork of God—to use the bishops' expression (#31)— unique among all creatures. This in itself is reason enough to accord respect.

Turning to the biblical tradition we discover two distinct descriptions of creation. These accounts originate from different periods of biblical Israel's history and in response to differing religious concerns. Still, the views of humankind in these two theological traditions are very similar.

The first tradition claims that we are creatures of the earth as are the fish of the sea, the birds of the air, the cattle and every creeping thing that creeps on the earth (Gn 1:26–28). The second and older one states that we were formed from the earth as were the rest of living things (Gn 2:7, 9, 19). They both insist that, unlike the rest of creation, there is another dimension to humankind that transcends the stuff of the earth. One tradition calls it the image/likeness of God (1:26–27). The second speaks of it as the breath of life (2:7).

With the ancients, we recognize that we are a mysterious composite of material and immaterial. The way we understand this combination has shaped our values, ordered our priorities, and influenced the way we live in our world.

We believe that we are made in the image and according to the likeness of God. But what does this mean? Is there a spark of the divine that enlivens us and is constantly trying to escape the confines of our bodies in order to be reunited with God? Or are we like God because some part of us—a soul—is supernatural? Is it perhaps that we have godlike powers? That we perform some godlike functions? Each one of these ideas has been offered by our tradition as an explanation of this mysterious image/likeness. It is true that they all have something in common. Still, each is very different from the other. Just what *is* the image/likeness of God?

There is no doubt that as human beings we enjoy certain abilities that are far superior to what we know the other animals possess. We can know; we can understand; we can stand in admiration of the wonders of creation and the wonderfulness of the creator. We can choose; we can follow fresh insights and devise creative ways of allowing them to flourish. We stand in the midst of creation, able to do what no other creature can do. We can think and decide; we can imagine and remember; we can shape and even transform ourselves and our world. We can consciously praise God. All of these abilities reflect the dignity that is ours as human beings, the dignity of which the bishops speak. It is no wonder that for many people any one or several of these abilities would constitute the image of God.

The Scriptures themselves tell us that we have been commissioned to subdue the earth and have dominion over the rest of creation (Gn 1:26, 28). Surely our superior abilities give us the right, perhaps even the duty, to rule the world. Some people believe that it is precisely in such domination that the meaning of image of God is to be found.

The Responsibility That Is Ours

There is another way of understanding this mysterious concept, a way that is closer to its original meaning. In the ancient Near Eastern world, the world of biblical Israel, people would set up an image of a monarch or of a god to represent the place where that royal or divine ruler was supreme. The image was not itself an idol. It was a symbol, and it symbolized not the ruler but the reign. It functioned much like a national flag does today. It represented sovereignty and jurisdiction.

We cannot deny that at times the people of the ancient world failed to distinguish between the symbol and that which it symbolized. This explains why what was intended as a sign of something else frequently deteriorated into an idol that was worshipped. Still, image as symbol is most likely the meaning intended in the creation narrative.

We read that as creatures we inherit this earth along with the fish of the sea, the birds of the air, and every living thing that moves upon the earth (Gn 1:26, 28). But we, and only we, are images of God. We alone are signs of divine sovereignty. As images we represent how and where *God* reigns supreme. As images we have the responsibility of fulfilling the role that *God* would fulfill. As images we must subdue and have dominion in the way that *God* would subdue and have dominion. Of all the creatures of the universe, we stand as unique signs and instruments of God's reign. The question of our superiority over other creatures is really a question of the manner of God's reign through us. We are the "faithful stewards in caring for the earth" (#32).

It would seem that God's will for the world is that it "be fertile, multiply, and fill the water of the seas . . . and the earth" (Gn 1:22). It would seem that our dignity and responsibility as God's images is to see that this is accomplished. Since the earth itself appears to possess an inner urgency that strains toward this goal, we do not have to induce it. What we must do is safeguard it. In the second creation account the human being was placed in the garden to cultivate it and to care for it (Gn 2:15).

As we test and probe and experiment, as we alter and redirect and fashion, as we subdue and have dominion, we must cherish the earth, nurture its fruitfulness and foster its growth. We can, indeed we must, exercise control over the earth, but this must be in accord with the life processes that are operative within its very heart. "To stand before God as the creator is to respect God's creation . . ." (#34).

We alone of all the creatures of the earth can take hold of the powers of creation and reshape them for our own advancement. We alone have discovered fire and have harnessed the energies of water, and of the wind, and of the sun, and of the atom. As images of God, we walk through our world with dignity and authority, but we must also walk with responsibility and trustworthiness. The earth is in our keeping. We hold its future well-being and survival in our hands. Possessing such power, we can never forget that as images of God we are stewards of the household of God.

A PEOPLE OF THE COVENANT

Most people, when they hear the word covenant, think either of the pact entered into at Mount Sinai or of the new relationship established by Jesus. But there is another relationship, another covenant, at the heart of creation. Once again it is the Book of Genesis that provides us with the tradition. God says to Noah:

> See, I am now establishing my covenant with you and your descendants after you and with every living creature with you: all the birds, and the various tame and wild animals with you.

According to the narrative, Noah and his family are the only survivors of the flood. Representing the entire human race, they are called into covenant with God. Not only this particular generation but every succeeding generation will participate in this pact. Not only humans but every living thing on earth, even the earth itself, will be secure because of this covenant.

At this point, it is important to make explicit the relationship between our environment and our economy. Ecosystem and economy are both combinations of "eco," which comes from the Greek *oikos*, meaning household. The earth is a storehouse or household of resources that we need and want. An ecosystem is the proper balance within this household between living things and their environment. Our environment or ecosystem is the household of resources within which we live. The management or law (*nomos*) of a household (*oikos*) is its economy. An economy is only appropriate if it is sensitive to the resources of the household as well as to the just distribution of these resources.

As individual as we may be, we are, nonetheless, members of a universal community. God, the entire human race, and all of creation are partners in this particular covenant. As covenant partner, God promised to preserve all living things, indeed, the earth itself. Never again would there be a flood to destroy the earth and the living things on it (Gn 9:11, 15). For its part, creation proceeds according to natural laws, thereby sustaining a certain ecological harmony. It seems that of all the partners of the covenant, it is only the descendants of Noah who must learn what fidelity to the covenant requires of them. Only they jeopardize environmental balance. Only they undermine social order. Only they stray from their commitment to God.

Stewardship Over

The earth is a storehouse of mineral and fossil treasures. Having discovered it, we are often captivated by its power. If we are responsible stewards we will manage the goods of the household lest we squander our treasure and it be lost to us forever. This treasure may well be used for our development, but not for our exploitation.

The earth vibrates with the pulsations of life, works miracles of renewal within the secrets of its body, and then feeds us with the fruits of these miracles. If we are responsible stewards we will be considerate about the strains that maturation can bear and be patient with its timing. The fruits of the earth are for our nourishment, but not for our hoarding.

Over the years and through the generations, the earth has been gorged and ravaged, polluted and stripped, and all the while it willingly offered its wealth asking only that this be taken with care and planning. We must discover what stewardship means. We must learn to reclaim the land, to purify the water, to freshen the air. Only then will the fish and the birds and everything that moves upon the earth "be fertile, multiply and fill the water of the seas . . . and the earth." We must learn this, or our environment will be destroyed and we will not survive as a race.

Stewardship With

A covenant relationship presumes certain attitudes: attitudes of mutual cooperation rather than unfair competition or arbitrary control; attitudes of genuine interdependence rather than restrictive dependence or disinterested independence; attitudes of unaffected respect and mutuality rather than unqualified dominance and submission.

It is to such covenantal attitudes that the bishops refer when they state that: "Biblical justice is more comprehensive than subsequent philosophical definitions. It is not concerned with a strict definition of rights and duties, but with the rightness of the human condition before God and within society" (#39).

The biblical vision proposed by the pastoral insists that respect for creation includes "both the world of nature and of human history" (#34). The goods of the household must be managed not only in the best interests of the earth, but also for the sake of *all* of the members of the household. Too often the generous earth has been captured and possessed by some of us to the exclusion of others. We cannot claim its riches as our own while some of our sisters and brothers languish in poverty. We cannot sate ourselves with its produce while others starve at our feet. We cannot amass and store what we will never be able to use while others wither away in desperation.

We have not yet learned to be stewards of God's earth. What possessions we have, we have in trust, to be distributed where there is need. The warmth, the comfort, the refreshment of the earth belong to everyone. As images of God, we merely manage this earth in God's name. "From the Patristic period to the present, the church has affirmed that misuse of the world's resources or appropriation of them by a minority of the world's population betrays the gift of creation since 'whatever belongs to God belongs to all'" (#34).

Stewardship means that we feed the hungry, give drink to the thirsty, clothe the naked. Without denying the human need to be somehow identified with a specific piece of land and to enjoy the rights that accompany this need, we must share the wealth of the earth or we will not survive as a society.

The earth has been given to *us*, not to *me* or to *you* but to *us*. We are equal partners in the covenant and we must share the earth and its riches with each other. Our relationship with the earth is a communal relationship. According to the narrative, Noah represented *all* of the people who were saved from destruction. This included his immediate family and the future generations as well. "I am now establishing my covenant with you and your descendants after you" (Gn 9:9).

This same idea introduces the section in the pastoral entitled "Food and Agriculture." 'The fundamental test of an economy is its ability to meet the essential human needs of this generation and future generations in an equitable fashion" (#216).

The earth unsparingly offers us food and drink with a liberality like that of God. No questions are asked; no one is turned away. Having been born into life is reason enough to be sustained. As images of God and stewards of the household, we must safeguard the fruitfulness and wealth of the earth and we must share this earth with all of creation, but most especially with each other.

Conclusion

The kind of economic justice envisioned by the bishops flows from an acknowledgement of the dignity of every human being as image of god. With this dignity comes the responsibility of the management of natural resources. Since all are creatures of the earth, all have the right to live from its riches. Since all are created in God's image, all have the right to participate in the management of these riches. A wise and just economic system will serve a vision such as this. A wise and just society will pursue "economic justice for all."

FURTHER READINGS

Birch, Bruce C., and Larry L. Rasmussen. *The Predicament of the Prosperous.* Philadelphia: Westminster, 1978.

Hessel, Dieter T., ed. *For Creation's Sake: Preaching, Ecology, & Justice.* Philadelphia: The Geneva Press, 1985.

Neal, Marie Augusta. *A Socio-Theology of Letting Go.* New York: Paulist Press, 1977.

Soelle, Dorothee, and Shirley A. Cloyes. *To Work and to Love: A Theology of Creation.* Philadelphia: Fortress Press, 1984.

QUESTIONS

1. In what ways do poverty and unemployment threaten the dignity that is ours as human beings "created in God's image"?

2. How do the traditions found in Genesis call us to both ecological stewardship and economic justice?

3. How can responsible stewardship influence the way we make use of our scientific advances in agriculture and technology?

4. Discuss the tensions between land and property rights (both national and international) and the right of every human being to have what is necessary for a life with dignity.

2

Community and Justice: A Biblical Perspective

Leslie J. Hoppe, O.F.M.

The biblical understanding of justice gives a fundamental per-spective to our reflections on social and economic justice. (#37)

Introduction: Can the Bible Help?

DESPITE THE CHRISTIAN BELIEF IN THE BIBLE AS THE WORD OF GOD, there are problems in allowing the perspectives of the Bible to shape our faith and life today. The world that produced the Bible is not our world. Some of the religious perspectives of the biblical tradition seem so foreign. For example, the stories about God's "interventions" in Israel's life do not seem to ring true to con-temporary experience. Our society bears little resemblance to any of the ancient Israelite social systems. One wonders whether and to what extent an ethic that was useful to nomads or to the early tribes or to people living under Israel's kings could be of any real help today. Ancient Israel's economic system was far less complex than that of even the most underdeveloped coun-tries today. If indeed the world of ancient Israel differs so much from our world, how can the Bible help Christians today hear God's call in their lives?

Despite the vast differences between our world and that of the Bible, there are a number of values which remain constant. One of these is the determination of believers to make their decisions in accordance with the "will of God" especially as that will has been revealed. A good portion of the Bible presents itself as the revelation of the divine will. In fact, the Bible begins with "the Law," which is a comprehensive declaration of God's will.

The Law of God

When the Bible speaks about the Law of God, the context is ancient Israel's belief that it was specially called by God to obedience. This God who called Israel to obedience was the very God who delivered Israel from bondage in Egypt. The Law of God as presented in the Bible is concerned with giving shape to Israel's response to God's gift of freedom. More than any other biblical text, the Book of Deuteronomy stresses that Israel is a special entity obligated in a special way to obedience. The Law of God then is addressed to Israel as a people, a community, a nation. It does not take the individual as its point of departure. It is the community which is to be holy because the Lord is holy (Lv 19:2). While the Law of God is addressed to the community, it, of course, applies to the individual members of that community, yet ancient Israelite ethics is not concerned about individual self-realization. Even the Decalogue (Ex 20; Dt 5), which does address the individual, makes its appeal for obedience in the context of a call to all Israel. In the Bible there is no individual morality that is to be distinguished from responsibility in and for the community. As a result, the test which determines the morality of a particular course of action is not the good will or good intention of the individual nor the nature of the action itself but the effect that it may have in the concrete community life of Israel.

For example, the eighth commandment ("You shall not bear dishonest witness against your neighbor." [Dt 5:20]) does not forbid lying in general nor is it based on any abstract notion of truth. It deals with the concrete situation of the judicial process. It forbids saying anything that would pervert the justice that God requires of Israel. The truth must be spoken not because lying is intrinsically evil but because truthful evidence is needed if justice is to be done to one's neighbor. The focus of the commandment is on the people who will be affected by the truth of falsehood that will be spoken in court. The bishops recognize the relationship between law and community in ancient Israel when they write: "Far from being an arbitrary restriction on the life of the people, these codes made life in community possible" (#36).

Biblical Justice

It is clear then that one component of the divine will as revealed to Israel is that the people ought to exist in harmony and that the community of Israel ought to be characterized by justice. In this context, justice is not giving to individuals their due; rather, justice is what creates, maintains, and enhances community life. Injustice is any action which destroys that life. Here is where there is a striking difference between contemporary American perspectives and those of the Bible. In today's society there is an emphasis on the individual. The rights of the individual must be protected. The ideal society is one which provides an atmosphere for the actualization of the individual's full potential. Even concern for others is seen as an expression of the individual's virtue. For the ancient Israelites life was a network of relationships. Fidelity to the divine will is presented as fidelity to those relationships. If Israel will obey the divine will, its society will be marked by justice which is understood as fidelity to community. It is this fidelity which is the true indicator of the state of Israel's relationship with God.

Trying to summarize the biblical view of justice and community in the space alloted for this essay is not really possible. The present essay will take just one of ancient Israel's laws (the law of release in Deuteronomy 15:1–11) and see how it reflects the biblical perspective on the justice that ought to characterize the community. The bishops cite the law as an example of ancient Israelite legislation that attempted to ensure social and economic justice within the community: "Laws such as that for the sabbath year when the land was left fallow (Ex 23:11; Lv 25:1–7) and for the year of release of debts (Dt 15:1–11) . . . reminded Israel that as a people freed by God from bondage they were to be concerned for the poor and oppressed in their midst" (#36).

The Law of Release: Deuteronomy 15:1–11

A basic Israelite belief was that though God gave the land to Israel, it really belonged to the Lord who gave it as a gift to Israel in accordance with the promises made to Israel's ancestors (Dt

11:8–12). An important consequence of this belief was a recognition of Israel's dependence upon God's bounty. The wealthy and the poor alike were to acknowledge God as the source of their sustenance. One way that Israel chose to express this belief was through the customs surrounding the year of release.

This law owes its origin to the custom of allowing the land to lie fallow at regular intervals (see Ex 23:10–11 and Lv 25:1–7). Obviously, the observance of such a custom would have been staggered throughout Israel, but each time it was observed by an individual farmer, the fallow year made life difficult for those economically dependent upon agriculture. Certainly they would have found repaying any outstanding debts extremely difficult. One purpose of the forerunner of the Deuteronomic law was to prohibit the calling in of debts during a farmer's fallow year though Deuteronomy required that the debt be forgiven rather than simply deferred. Ancient Israel's laws make it clear that no one was to take advantage of another's financial difficulties. The poor were to experience the generosity of their fellow Israelites.

Deuteronomy's Re-interpretation of an Ancient Law

Because of the practical problems associated with the observance of the fallow year, this custom fell into disuse. Nowhere does Deuteronomy make any mention of the fallow or sabbath year though the legislation in Exodus and Leviticus still refers to that ancient custom. Deuteronomy, in a real sense, updates an ancient law by breaking its ties with a no longer observed agricultural custom while retaining its concern for those with financial problems. More than this, Deuteronomy tries to eliminate the possibility of a debtor class in the Israelite community by requiring the cancellation of all debts owed by one Israelite to another at the end of every seventh year. Deuteronomy then is not just calling for charity but it is trying to insure that Israelite society will not be divided *permanently* into two classes: the economically powerful and the economically dependent.

The kind of loans that this Deuteronomic law has in mind is one which involved the pledge of personal services as security against nonpayment. Apparently creditors were within their legal rights to compel delinquent debtors to become bond servants in the case of default. Deuteronomy not only requires that the debt be cancelled but in effect it also frees those who had become bond servants in order to work off their debts. So that the source of loans to the poor would not dry up, the law enjoins people of means to lend to those in need even as the year of release approached (15:8). Failure to be generous to the poor is described as an evil with the use of the formula: ". . . you will be held guilty" (15:9b). Deuteronomy uses the same formula to condemn the withholding of the wages of the poor (see 24:15b). The assumption behind this negative motivation is that help for the poor should be forthcoming from the people of means. Any failure in this regard brings divine judgment upon the Israelite community since God is the defender of the poor.

The Motives for Obedience

After the law of release is given in verses 1–3, there follows a description of the blessings that will come to Israel if this law is observed (vv. 4–6). The result of compliance will be nothing less than the elimination of poverty in the land which was Israel's inheritance from God: ". . . there should be no one of you in need." (v. 4) Also Israel's prosperity will be such that it can offer loans to other nations (Dt 15:6). God will provide for Israel's material needs in such a way that poverty need not exist if only Israel were obedient. This approach is typical of Deuteronomy which does not simply state laws which are to be observed but also seeks to move its readers to obedience by providing motives for observance.

Another typically Deuteronomic characteristic is the assumption that *all Israelites* belong to *one family*. This passage refers to the poor as "kinsmen" of the wealthy no less than six times in the eleven verses that make up the law of release (vv. 2, 3, 7 [2x], 9, 11). That some members of the one family of Israel be without the material blessings promised to all is just not right according to Deuteronomy. Of course, the authors of this text were realistic enough to recognize that the kind of obedience needed to bring an end to poverty would not be forthcoming from Israel. That is why the book calls so strongly for generosity toward the poor: ". . . I command you to open your hand to your poor and needy kinsmen in your country" (v. 11). Deuteronomy fails to find any positive value in poverty. It is never described as a state which places one in closer proximity to God; rather, the deprivation of material blessings enjoyed by the wealthy was an evil which must be eliminated by means of generous actions on the part of people who themselves savored these blessings.

This law makes it clear that Deuteronomy understands the poor person as one without the kind of material prosperity that allows for economic security. The poor are those who need the economic support of others. Occasionally the needs of the poor became so acute that they were forced into bond slavery by their creditors. Such a situation was not to become permanent within the Israelite community, otherwise a socio-economic rift would develop within that community which could destroy it. Deuteronomy envisions a community whose members understand themselves as members of a single family and act accordingly. Such an attitude and behavior could effectively eliminate poverty in the Israelite community.

The Failure to Obey

Finally in characterizing the unwillingness to aid the poor as a sin (v. 9), Deuteronomy asserts that Israel's relationship with God was a product of the intersocietal relationships that existed among the Israelites themselves. Traditions with a more pronounced cultic orientation like those behind the Books of Chronicles seem to assume that Israel's relationship with God was determined by ritual activity. While Deuteronomy does not ignore liturgical approach to the Divine, it chooses to emphasize a view of religion that sees the relationship between God and Israel as determined by the quality of human relationships among the Israelites themselves. This approach to religion seems paradoxical but it is no more so than the promise that the enjoyment of the land and its material blessings rests upon the readiness of the wealthy to relinquish them (vv. 4–6, 10).

Conclusion

This essay began with the question regarding the value of biblical insights for contemporary moral issues. The Deuteronomic law of release was chosen precisely because it shows that fidelity to the biblical tradition does not require that one blindly apply ancient laws to the contemporary situation. The Deuteronomists reinterpret what was already for them an ancient and impractical custom. The values which the Deuteronomists wished to preserve, despite changing economic and social conditions, are values that ought to be preserved by believers today as well. The most important of these is the recognition that both rich and poor belong to the same family. This familial relationship itself ought to give a clear indication of what justice means. Second is the acknowledgment that the earth's bounty belongs to no one absolutely. It is a gift given by God to all the people. Third is the recognition that poverty and want just do not happen; they are the result of people's unwillingness to obey the divine will. If people are obedient poverty would not exist.

The difference of perspectives between our world and that which produced the Bible does not merely reflect the different socio-economic conditions between ancient Israel and contemporary American society. They also show that the values of our society are not shaped by the biblical tradition as much as they ought to be. Certainly our society would be much different if we really believed that all people belong to one family and that the earth's bounty is a gift that God has given to us all and that our right relationship with God is one product of just intersocietal relationships.

FURTHER READINGS

Haughey, John C., ed. *The Faith That Does Justice.* New York: Paulist Press, 1977.
Mott, Stephen Charles. *Biblical Ethics and Social Change.* New York: Oxford University Press, 1982.
Schrey, H.H. *The Biblical Doctrine of Justice and Law.* London: SCM Press, 1955.

QUESTIONS

1. What values from the biblical tradition can help contemporary societies deal with issues of justice?

2. What practical conclusions can Christians draw from the assumption of the Deuteronomist that all Israel forms a single family?

3. What is the biggest obstacle facing Christians today as they try to act in accordance with justice understood as that which promotes fidelity to the community?

4. Does Deuteronomy (see 15:4, 11) consider poverty as inevitable?

3

Option For The Poor: Old Testament Directives

Carroll Stuhlmueller, C.P.

THE U.S. BISHOPS PRESENT THEIR PASTORAL MESSAGE ON
Economic Justice for All as "a personal invitation to American
Catholics to use the resources of our faith . . . to shape a society
which better protects the dignity and basic rights of our sisters
and brothers both in this land and around the world" (Pastoral
Message #2). In response we turn to one of the major resources
of faith, the Hebrew Scriptures, "to lift up the human and ethical
dimensions of economic life" (Pastoral Message #7). In the initial
section the title of this chapter, "Option for the Poor," turns into
a question of conscience, *Is it really an option?* Next we ask: *Who
are the poor?* Then we investigate how Israel, the chosen one of
the Hebrew Scriptures, is *a people poor and afflicted by definition.*
Paradoxically in the final section we see that Israel is *a people
blessed with land and abundance,* and here we must ask, *How do
we properly make use of these lavish gifts?*

Is it Really an Option?

The answer to this question must be "Yes," because poor and
helpless people cannot force anyone to pay attention to them.
The *ani* (sg.) or *anawim* (pl.), the classic Hebrew word for the
poor, simply do not possess the financial means nor the social
prestige, frequently enough not the educational opportunities

nor the political base, to require others to intervene and help them.

From the viewpoint of faith, however, people do not possess the option to decide (or not) to assist others in need. Even God, infinitely free, did not feel this kind of choice towards Israel in slavery and destitution. God would have been justified in ignoring these people, at least according to our calculations, because of their repeated infidelity, even grieving God's holy spirit as Isaiah wrote (Is 63:10). God, however, reacted differently and in a paroxysm of divine passion declared through the prophet Hosea:

> How could I give you up, O Ephraim,
>   or deliver you up, O Israel? . . .
> My heart is overwhelmed,
>   my pity is stirred.
> I will not give vent to my blazing anger,
>   I will not destroy Ephraim again;
> For I am God, and not man,
>   the Holy One present among you. (Hos 11:8–9)

Nor could Jesus give up on the poor. He gravitated towards them in his ministry, even to be with them for rest and relaxation. While preaching or praying at Jerusalem, Jesus was accustomed to spend the night at the suburban village of Bethany, which in Hebrew, *beth-ani,* means "house of the poor." Bethany was the closest place to Jerusalem, where lepers could come and gaze prayerfully upon the holy city and its sacred buildings (cf. Mk 14:3).

Poverty, whatever be the cause, economic, physical, or social, is almost like leprosy, for it puts an awkward distance between the poor and their brothers and sisters better off than themselves. Sometimes too these more affluent brothers and sisters erect their own protective barriers against the poor by questioning the causes of their destitution and blaming it on irresponsibility or sloth. We think at once of Jesus' answer to the question, "Who sinned?" about the blind man "who used to sit and beg." He declared:

> It was no sin, either of this man or of his parents. Rather, it was to let God's works show forth in him. (Jn 9:3)

Sin and blame also evoked the Solomonic reply of Jesus:

> Let the one among you who has no sin be the first to throw a stone at her. (Jn 8:7)

Called to be a compassionate person like God in the Hebrew Scriptures and like Jesus the Messiah, we have no other option than to respond to the outcry and affliction of the poor. A prophetic imperative brings pressure upon our conscience. This response is not a call to a more sublime holiness, which we can accept or reject and still be saved in our mediocre state. Rather, it is a summons to salvation whose only other option is disassociation from the poor and therefore from the Messiah Jesus. Put plainly and severely, in typical prophetic style, the only option is salvation or damnation in caring for or disregarding the poor.

The Poor, Who Are They?

Poverty, in the Scriptures, is not a simple matter of sloth or sin. In fact, *anawim* becomes an important theological word in the Bible. We need to study this word more carefully, to realize the expectation placed upon our conscience.

Anawim begins to acquire a specific religious meaning with the prophet Zephaniah. The prophet is addressing the remnant of the people who survived "a day of wrath, . . . of anguish and distress" (Zep 1:14–15).

> Seek the Lord, all you humble (*anawim*)
> of the earth,
> who have observed the law.
> Seek justice, seek humility,
> perhaps, you may be sheltered
> on the day of the Lord's anger. (2:3)

Poverty and sorrow turn the people's mind back to God and to observance of the law. The poor exemplify a humble attitude and become the heralds of the good news for everyone else.

These poor people are not only the remnant of the old Israel but they are also the seed and ovum of the new Israel. Zephaniah declared:

> I will leave as a remnant in your midst
>   a people humble and lowly,
> Who shall take refuge in the name of the Lord:
>   the remnant of Israel. (3:12)

The phrase, "a people humble and lowly," in its ancient Greek translation, inspired Jesus' lovely invitation:

> "Come to me, all you who labor and are burdened, and I will give you rest. Take my yoke upon you and learn from me, for I am meek and humble of heart; and you will find rest for yourselves. For my yoke is easy, and by burden light." (Mt 11:28–30)

Jesus was so identified with the poor that they came to exemplify the way of messianic salvation. This development is not surprising if we recall the announcement of another prophet, Zechariah:

> See, your king shall come to you;
>   a just savior is he,
> *Meek (ani)*, and riding on an ass. (Zec 9:9)

These prophetical passages inspire major portions of the bishops' pastoral on *Economic Justice for All*. They themselves admit that "we write as heirs of the biblical prophets" (Pastoral Message #4).

Israel, Poor and Afflicted in Its Origin

The prophets, we have seen, identify Israel as "the remnant . . . a people humble and lowly" (Zep 3:12). It is helpful to reach behind the prophets, as they themselves did, into the early traditions about the origins of Israel in poverty and helplessness.

Recalling the first days of Israel, Micah pleads:

> O my people, what have I done to you,
>   or how have I wearied you? Answer me!
> For I brought you up from the land of Egypt,
>   From the place of slavery I released you. (Mi 6:3–4)

This passage of Micah concludes with the famous prophetic Torah or Law:

> You have been told, o man, what is good,
>   and what the Lord requires of you:
> Only to do the right and to love goodness,
>   and to walk humbly with your God. (Mi 6:8)

If, with the prophets, we search for Israel in its earliest days, we will discover their true identity. In God's initial call to this people we will learn the divine definition of what made them "my special possession, dearer to me than all other people" (Ex 19:6). Over and over God meets a people in serious need, poor and dependent, without social or racial identity.

Abraham and Sarah were part of a large migration of Asiatic people, who had been forced out of Ur of the Chaldees in modern southern Iraq (Gn 11:31). God turned this political and social necessity into an inaugural call to become the parents of the chosen people and the source of blessings for all nations (Gn 12:2–3). For many years Abraham and Sarah were childless (Gn 15:1–6), merely resident aliens in that very land promised to them by God (Gn 23). Their offspring migrated into Egypt, where a later king "reduced them to cruel slavery, making life bitter for them with hard work, . . . the whole cruel fate of slaves" (Ex 1:13–14).

God intervened, appearing to Moses and declaring to him:

I have witnessed the affliction of my people in Egypt and have heard their cry of complaint against their slave drivers, so I know well what they are suffering. Therefore I have come down to rescue them from the hands of the Egyptians. (Ex 3:7–8)

This new beginning identifies Israel as a group of disheartened, beaten slaves, and for that very reason the object of God's compassion and intervention.

The people who fled or were driven from Egypt (Ex 3:20; 6:1; 10:28; 14:5) could not pride themselves even on a pure bloodstream, for we learn in Exodus 12:38 and Numbers 11:4 that they included "a crowd of mixed ancestry" and "foreign elements." The Hebrew terms here (*ereb rab* and *asapsup*) could just as easily be translated "riffraff," to fit the sound of the Hebrew. "They grumbled against Moses" (Ex 15:24) and hankered for "the cucumbers, the melons, the leeks, the onions, and the garlic" of Egypt (Nm 11:5). Even Moses had his moment of doubt and was prevented from entering the promised land (Nm 20:7–13).

Deuteronomy sums up the origin and underlying characteristics of Israel:

> It was not because you are the largest of all nations that the Lord set his heart on you and chose you, for you are really the smallest of all nations. It was because the Lord loved you and because of his fidelity to the oath he had sworn to your fathers, that he brought you out with his strong hand from the place of slavery. (Dt 7:7–8)

This definition of Israel is matched by God's definition of himself.

At the beginning of the Ten Commandments God will be identified: "I, the Lord, am your God, who brought you out of the land of Egypt, that place of slavery" (Ex 20:2; Dt 5:6).

When Moses wanted to see the face of God—impossible for "no one sees me and still lives" (Ex 33:20; cf. Is 6:5)—God replied by passing by Moses on Mount Sinai and proclaiming:

> The Lord, the Lord, a merciful and gracious God, slow to anger and rich in kindness and fidelity, continuing his kindness for a thousand generations, and forgiving wickedness and crime and sin; yet not declaring the guilty guiltless. (Ex 34:6–7)

God takes a responsible attitude towards sin, but all the while promises that mercy far outstrips punishment.

God thus proclaimed his name and revealed the divine presence while Moses stood on Mount Sinai, holding in his arms the two tablets of the law or the ten commandments. The bishops' pastoral comments upon this scene:

> The codes of Israel reflect the norms of the covenant: reciprocal responsibility, mercy and truthfulness. They embody a life of freedom from oppression: worship of the One God, rejection of idolatry, mutual respect among people, care and protection for every member of the social body. Being free and being a co-responsible community are God's intentions for us. (#36)

By definition, therefore, Israel was a people poor and insignificant in its origins, the object of God's compassion. Equally by definition, moreover, Israel was a people, sinful and unworthy yet divinely endowed with freedom, human dignity and a future messianic salvation beyond all expectation. At the heart of the covenant was that dual spirit of responsibility and compassion. No one can claim citizenship in Israel without a strong commitment to these norms.

Israel, Blessed with Land and Abundance

Israel is equally defined as a people with a promise, and for our study right now, the promise of land. Before Moses died, God led him up Mount Nebo, overlooking the entire country, and declared:

> This is the land which I swore to Abraham, Isaac and Jacob that I would give to their descendants. I have let you feast your eyes upon it, but you shall not cross over. (Dt 34:4)

Land was a place of promise but it also had its conditions, even for someone as great as Moses.

The land was never given unconditionally to the people, as we learn in another important passage:

> The land shall not be sold in perpetuity; for the land is mine, and you are but aliens who have become my tenants. Therefore, in every part of the country that you occupy, you must permit the land to be redeemed. (Lv 25:23–24)

The land was held in trust from God, and the major condition lay in the expectation that no family ever be deprived permanently of their homestead. At least every fifty years each one possessed the God-given right to return to the family portion. The bishops remark about this passage of Leviticus, quoting from Pope John Paul II: "Whatever belongs to God belongs to all" (#34).

When land was stolen, even by kings, prophets spoke out fiercely, as in the well-known incident of Naboth's vineyard (1 Kgs 21). The prophet Micah, from the small village of Moresheth, enunciated words drenched with tears and burning with anguish, as he excoriated powerful, greedy people:

> They covet fields, and seize them;
>   houses, and they take them;
> They cheat an owner of his house,
>   a man of his inheritance. (Mi 2:2)
> The women of my people you drive out
>   from their pleasant houses;
> From their children you take away
>   forever the honor I gave them. (Mi 2:9)

We are reminded of what we Americans have inflicted upon the Native Americans by the outrageous seizure of their land and the cruel relocation of them in tribal reservations (see #7).

Land and all its riches are provided for the way of salvation, for justice, meekness and innocence, for human dignity and family integrity. As anyone goes to sleep at night, he or she ought to be able to dream—and in waking hours to seek—the vision of the prophet Isaiah about the promised Messiah. First he shall "judge the poor with justice and decide aright for the land's afflicted." Then we perceive how:

> The wolf shall be a guest of the lamb,
>   and the leopard shall lie down with the kid.
> The baby shall play by the cobra's den,
>   and the child lay his hand on the adder's
>   lair.
> There shall be no harm or ruin on all my holy
>   mountain;
>   for the earth shall be filled with the
>   knowledge of the Lord. (Is 11:6,8,9)

Only when land is received with the hope of achieving this prophetic dream will the land be rightly retained. So long as there are destitute and fearful families without the dignity and warmth of their home, everyone's land is in jeopardy.

Conclusion

There is no option for the poor except to share with them and to receive the gift of their humble meekness within our soul and so to be identified with the Messiah Jesus. The *anawim* or poor is a title for the messianic people and for Messiah. Only by bonding with the poor do we authentically find membership with the chosen people Israel who by definition are people in need—of God and of one another—in a family of compassion. To these people the greatest promises are given; to them the gift of land and its rich produce belong, but only if the land is received as a loan from God, and this on condition that no one is without land, food, and employment.

Further Readings

Avila, Rafael. *Worship and Politics*. Maryknoll: Orbis Books, 1981.

Gelin, Albert. *The Poor of Yahweh*. Collegeville: The Liturgical Press, 1964.

Roy, Leon. "Poor." In *Dictionary of Biblical Theology*, edited by Xavier Leon-Dufour. 2d ed. New York: Seabury, 1973, pp. 436–438.

Schiblin, Richard. *The Bible, the Church, and Social Justice*. Liguori Publications, 1983.

Tamez, Elsa. *Bible of the Oppressed*. Maryknoll: Orbis Books, 1982.

Questions

1. From rereading Genesis 12:1–6; chapter 17; and Exodus 3 describe the background of the chosen people Israel. Who are under similar circumstances today and qualify as God's chosen people?

2. Chapter 11 of Hosea is often referred to as an anguished cry of divine passion. Yet chapters 2–3 of Micah portray God as experiencing a different kind of passion, this time of anger over the mistreatment of the poor. Comparing these chapters with Exodus 34, how do we best understand the character or attitude of God?

3. Biblical passages like Isaiah 41:17–20 or 43:1–7, along with the earlier prophecy of Zephaniah, give us different glimpses of the poor. How do the poor provide an image of the people who belong to the messianic kingdom?

4

Called To Be Disciples

Donald Senior, C.P.

A KEY BIBLICAL IDEA DEVELOPED IN THE BISHOPS' PASTORAL IS THAT
of "discipleship." It is one of the New Testament's most powerful
motifs and in this chapter I would like to spell out in more detail
some of its meaning and its connection with economic justice.

Discipleship: Key Gospel Motif
   The bishops underscore that Jesus gathered his first followers
into a community of disciples (#47). The Greek term for "disciple" (*matheteus*) means literally a "learner" or "student." Discipleship was a common mode of education in the ancient world.
The Greek philosophers gathered disciples who followed their
masters and learned wisdom from them. So, too, did students
eager to learn the meaning of the Jewish law and searching for
the compassion and prudence needed to interpret it well seek
out rabbis or teachers. The Bible has always known famous
"teacher-disciple" relationships such as that of Moses and
Aaron, or Elijah and Elisha.
   But this form of personalized education or mentoring takes on
particular importance as presented in the Gospels. The disciples
that Jesus gathers and forms into a fragile community represent
not only those historical figures who followed the teacher from
Nazareth but, for the Christian reader of the Gospels, the dis-

29

ciples reflect the hopes and difficulties of Christians in every age. Discipleship becomes a metaphor for describing our whole relationship with Christ as a community of believers. Discipleship is not a temporary stage for Christians, with graduation moving us on to professional rank. We are always "learners" in the school of faith, constantly plumbing the depth of our relationship with Christ, constantly stumbling along the mysterious journey of faith. All of us, lay, religious, clergy, are beginners in the school of Jesus. It is important, therefore, on the issue of economic justice—as with every challenge to authentic Christian life—to carefully review the meaning of discipleship as portrayed in the Gospels.

The bishops' pastoral provides a fine discussion of discipleship, particularly in paragraphs #45–52. There are five elements in the Gospel portrayal of discipleship that I would like to highlight. All of them are mentioned in the pastoral letter but not always in the order I will present them here. Our leads can be taken not only from the pastoral letter but from the Gospel passages to which the bishops allude. For example, the first encounter of Jesus with his disciples, found in Mark 1:16–20 (cited by the bishops in #45), provides an excellent starting point for our reflections:

> As he passed by the Sea of Galilee, Jesus saw Simon and his brother Andrew casting their nets into the sea; they were fishermen. Jesus said to them, "Come after me, I will make you fishers of men." Then they left their nets and followed him. He walked along a little farther and saw James, the son of Zebedee, and his brother John. They too were in a boat mending their nets. Then he called them. So they left their father Zebedee in the boat along with the hired men and followed him.

Discipleship as Call

This Gospel story makes it clear that being a disciple of Jesus is not a career choice but a personal call. As in the case of the fishermen of Galilee, it can come unexpectedly into our lives and completely disrupt what we normally do. For others it can be a more gradual process, a slow awakening to the meaning of the

Gospel for our lives. In every instance the call to follow Jesus is a gift of God, a "grace" in the full sense of the term. Something that is meant to reach down into the very depths of our being and affect every aspect of our life.

When we are called by someone we can either fall silent and turn away, or we can respond. The personal categories of call and response are important when considering the implications of Christian discipleship, including its meaning for economic justice. Following Jesus does not entail only one aspect of our life; being a disciple touches everything about us—our values, our choices, our resources, our dreams. Therefore we can expect changes and challenges once the call to be a disciple of Jesus has been heard and if we choose to respond to it.

Following Jesus

The bishops declare: "Discipleship involves imitating the pattern of Jesus' life by openness to God's will in the service of others" (#47). This gets at the heart of the matter. The intrinsic meaning of discipleship is the notion of "following"; the disciple shapes his or her life on that of the master or mentor. "Follow me"—those two words from the Gospel story above distill the essence of Christian life.

Obviously "following" or "imitiating" Jesus does not mean simply copying the surface details of his life, such as wearing first century garb or becoming an itinerant preacher. Imitating Jesus, as the bishops suggest, means that Christians are to shape their own lives in the pattern of Jesus. This is no simple process nor is there only one way of expressing the pattern of Christ's life in our own. Here is where the authentic disciple becomes a true learner by constanting reflecting on the teaching and example of Jesus and trying to see their meaning in our everyday lives. The bishops do this in their letter, singling out some of the most important aspects of Jesus' life and mission, especially as they touch issues of economic justice.

Jesus announced the nearness of God's reign (#41), a reign in which the gifts of creation are not exploited but reverenced and shared, where human beings are treated as children of God, where oppression and injustice are expunged, where the sick are healed, where the disabled are not excluded but have full access to the community, where those pushed to the margins are drawn into the heart of the community, where emnity and violence are replaced by reconciliation and love.

The Gospels illustrate that the Reign of God was not some romantic utopian ideal for Jesus or beautiful words spoken without cost but rather something he embodied in his own life and mission. "What Jesus proclaims by word, he enacts in his ministry" (#42). Each of the evangelists portrays a Jesus consumed with compassion, a tireless healer who was willing to break social and religious taboos to carry out his mission. The sick and dispossessed were drawn to him like a magnet and several times the Gospels describe compelling scenes as scores of the sick streamed toward Jesus seeking to be healed. Jesus was not afraid to risk his own reputation—and ultimately his own safety—in order to affirm the dignity of the marginalized and to draw them into the center of his community. He invited the hated tax collector Levi to be a disciple and welcomed the bold affection of a public sinner in Simon's house. The detested Samaritans become the heroes of his stories. He included women among his disciples in an age and culture when women had no public status. Nor did he fear to meet and even praise Gentiles who were regarded as enemies of his people.

In what he said and what he did Jesus embodied the values of God's Reign. "Following Jesus" means absorbing that same inclusive, compassionate, and just vision of the human family. Economic realities are hardly peripheral to this, as the bishops' pastoral letter constantly affirms. It would surely be empty religious rhetoric if the ministry of Jesus were construed solely in private, personal terms. Following the will of Jesus, without fail, leads to the hard realities of budgets and employment and allotment of resources. It ultimately involves the Christian in political debate and public process.

This, too, has an explicit biblical basis. In their letter the bishops focus on the Gospel of Luke, the evangelist who seems to give the most attention to economic realities (#48–49). Jesus is portrayed as a prophet who challenges the community of Israel, particularly the rich and powerful, to remember their covenant with God, a covenant calling for the sharing of resources with the poor and defenseless. Like the great prophets before him, Jesus' challenge was disturbing and met fierce, death-dealing opposition. Jesus' death on the cross is the ultimate sign of his message: a life poured out in love for others. It is also the sign that looms ahead in every disciple's journey: following Jesus is not without cost. The way of discipleship can become the way of the cross.

Change of Heart

The compelling beauty of the reign of God and the challenge it poses for many of our values and assumptions lead to another crucial dimension of discipleship. In the story quoted above, we are told that the disciples left everything—father, hired hands, home, boats, livelihood—and followed Jesus. This narrative illustrates what Jesus himself had declared immediately before encountering those Galilean fishermen: "The reign of God is at hand! Reform your lives and believe in the Gospel" (Mk 1:15). The Gospel assumes that becoming a disciple of Jesus and attempting to live by the values of God's reign will mean changes in the way we think and act. It will mean "repentance." The Greek term used for this in the Gospel is *metanoia*. Literally it means a "change of mind" or "change of perspective." That is an apt description of what has to happen if the Gospel is to take root in our lives—we need to change our perspective. Not "perspective" in a superficial sense but a change in our entire view of things, looking at reality through the values and vision of human life expressed in the Gospel.

Achieving economic justice, as the bishops's letter continually emphasizes, is not a matter of social or political manipulation. The chronic poverty of the developing nations, the lack of employment opportunities for the poor and minorities of this nation, the scandal of those who are rich at the expense of the needy—these injustices will not be solved merely by finding the right economic formula. Economic justice, as one fundamental dimension of the Gospel, will demand "repentance," a change of perspective. For many it could involve a substantial "leaving behind" of a level of affluence to which they have grown deeply attached.

Some of the cries of anger that greeted the various drafts of the bishops' pastoral came from people who had serious and legitimate differences of opinion on how to analyze and solve the problems of the U.S. economy. But some were cries of protest from those who instinctively know that achieving the kind of justice called for in the Gospel would involve a change of heart and a change of life they are unwilling to begin.

A Community of Disciples

The story of Jesus' meeting with the disciples along the shore of Galilee reflects another profound assumption about biblical discipleship. To be a disciple means life within a *community*. Jesus' first disciples were called as a group and would be sent on mission in groups.

Unlike modern western culture that prizes individualism, the biblical world gave first emphasis to the community—whether the family or the clan or the entire nation. The individual's worth and purpose had to be worked out within a community context. The value of individual dignity and rights treasured in our culture is also legitimate but it does not prepare us as well to deal with economic realities which are profoundly communitarian in nature. Catholic social teaching gives strong emphasis to the common good, and here it captures a key biblical virtue.

Jesus was embued with this sense of community, of the profound interrelationships of people with each other and with God. This, of course, was part of the rich heritage of Judaism upon which Jesus drew. The people of Israel were bound with God and with each other through the covenant. The Jewish law expressed the reality of that covenant and demanded an acute sense of justice and responsibility, especially for the poor and defenseless. The dominant symbol Jesus used to describe his mission, the "reign of God," is a social and political symbol and is essentially communal in nature. Jesus himself did not work as some sort of Lone Ranger but gathered a community of disciples with whom he lived and taught and worked. His stories and teachings point to a restored community of Israel with lost sheep returned to the fold, alienated sons brought back home, people dealing with each other out of respect and truthfulness rather than out of lust or dishonesty.

This gives us a way of looking at the church itself. The pastoral quotes John Paul II who describes the church as "a community of disciples" (#46). Each member of the church is called to join with others in living out the Gospel. That is why, later in the pastoral letter, the bishops state that the church itself must be the foremost exponent of economic justice in the way it deals with its own members (#347). This sense of community is a Gospel value with tremendous importance for the future of the world; avid consumerism that feeds only its own appetite is directly counter to the way of Christian discipleship.

Fishing for People

Following Jesus means sharing in his mission. In the story of the first calling of disciples that mission is picturesquely described as "fishing for people." The prophet Jeremiah (16:16) speaks forcefully of the Lord sending out fishermen to snare people for God in the coming day of judgment. The image is also used by Habakkuk (2:14–15), again in a context of struggle and judgment. The fishing image in these biblical passages is not that of a lazy, hazy day of summer fishing by the old pond, but the chaos and struggle of storm churned sea.

In that sense it is an apt metaphor for the ministry of Jesus to which the disciples are called. Jesus' mission involved life and death and he, too, was a gatherer of people. His teaching and healing brought new life but it also involved struggle and conflict. To be a follower of Jesus does not mean simply gazing on the beauty of the Lord but being willing to live by his values and taking up his cause, the cause of justice.

The issues of economic justice are not peripheral to Christian life nor are they a mere option reserved for those with a taste for such issues. The bread and butter concerns of employment and housing, of a just wage, of trade policies and the fate of agriculture—these are profoundly Gospel issues. The first disciples, the bishops remind us (#45), were not mountaintop contemplatives but working people, and the call to be a follower of Jesus reached them in the marketplace. It is there that the mission of establishing the reign of God is to take place.

The Bible, including the theme of discipleship, does not provide economic policy, nor can it settle the necessary debate which the bishops' letter will hopefully provoke. It does, however, lay before us a profound vision of the life to which God calls us. It is up to modern disciples of Jesus, drawing on the wisdom of the Scriptures, the strength of our Catholic tradition, and the inventiveness of people of good will, to incarnate that biblical vision within the realities of life today.

FURTHER READINGS

Cassidy, Richard J., and Philip J. Scharper, eds. *Political Issues in Luke-Acts*. Maryknoll: Orbis, 1983. (A collection of essays on Luke's Gospel that provide further insight into the Gospel most used in the pastoral.)

Senior, D. *Jesus: A Gospel Portrait*. Dayton: Pflaum, 1975. (Offers a more detailed study of the mission of Jesus and the meaning of discipleship.)

The Bible Today, vol. 24, November 1986. Collegeville: The Liturgical Press. (The entire issue of this magazine deals with the Bible and economic issues; additional copies may be obtained from The Liturgical Press.

QUESTIONS

1. Do you think of your own Christian life as a following of Jesus? In what way do economic issues effect your discipleship?

2. How does the bishops' call for economic justice imply the need for a "change of heart" or "repentance"?

3. Does the notion of the church as a "community of disciples" ring true from your experience? What concretely does this mean?

4. In what ways do you connect your mission as a disciple of Jesus with economic issues?

THE ETHICAL
PERSPECTIVE

5

A Growing Tradition of Ethical Critique

John Pawlikowski, O.S.M.

IN THE OPENING PART OF THEIR PASTORAL LETTER ON THE U.S. ECON-
omy the bishops call our attention to the long history of Catholic
concern about economic justice. It is central to our biblical tradition. The strong statements of the Hebrew Prophets and the
witness and teaching of Jesus in the New Testament, the Sermon
on the Mount in particular, are integral to any authentic spirituality rooted in the biblical tradition. And the many statements
of the Second Vatican Council and recent popes, including John
Paul II, have powerfully reechoed this scriptural imperative (#8).
It is important to recall this Catholic tradition because some in
the church have wrongly believed that the present pastoral letter
represents an unprecedented intrusion into the realm of economic policy. This is patently false. While the current pastoral
letter represents the most developed statement to date by the
U.S. hierarchy in this area, it stands in continuity with a tradition
that it is as ancient as the notion of a divinely originated covenantal peoplehood with a special responsibility to make God's
face of justice and mercy a known and living reality throughout
humankind.

Other sections of this volume spell out the roots of the pastoral
in the Scriptures and in the official teaching of Catholicism at an
international level. Here we shall briefly examine another facet

of the Catholic legacy of moral critique of the economy, namely, the witness in word and action of the American church leadership, especially after the first papal encyclical *Rerum novarum* issued by Pope Leo XIII in 1893 gave the stamp of Catholic approval to union organizing. Unfortunately this legacy is not widely known among present-day American Catholics, nor is its profound impact on helping raise the Catholic working classes in this country from the grips of widespread poverty and economic exploitation sufficiently appreciated. It is one of the best kept secrets of American Catholicism. Yet non-Catholic historians such as James Hastings Nichols have said that in many ways it represents the best social action doctrine of any church in America. And Fr. Andrew Greeley has shown how this social doctrine "would inspire hundreds and perhaps even thousands of young Catholic progressive reformers, liberal and even radicals in the first half of the twentieth century. It would have no difficulty reconciling itself with some elements in the mainstream of American social reform. Its thought and action would represent one of the happier marriages between the Catholic Church and American society." (*The Catholic Experience*, p. 217)

From the time that Cardinal Gibbons of Baltimore took his strong stand in favor of the Knights of Labor, the church was publicly identified with the interests of the working class. As a result the American Catholic working class never became alienated from the church in the same way as its European counterparts. Histories of the U.S. labor movement have often pointed to the strong Catholic influence upon it as one of the principal reasons for its relatively moderate social philosophy and policies. The American hierarchy's involvement in the nation's economic matters began in earnest soon after the end of World War I. By that time the unionization movement in the United States was somewhat on a roll partially at least because of its endorsement by the bishops in the spirit of *Rerum novarum*. The war itself also contributed significantly to the labor movement's growing strength. Military conscription during the war made it necessary to open up the U.S. work force in an extensive way to women and children. At the conclusion of the conflict the nation faced the difficult problem of finding employment for the returning soldiers. An intensification of labor strife was the result.

Because so many Catholics were part of the blue collar class directly affected by this strife, the American bishops felt compelled to address the issues involved. They did so twice. The first time was through their Program of Social Reconstruction which was made public on Lincoln's birthday, 1919. The other was through a pastoral letter, appearing some seven months later, which applied the principles of *Rerum novarum* to an American context for the very first time. Unlike the 1986 pastoral these documents do not go into the theological and biblical foundations for economic justice. Nor do they try to delineate any specific Catholic social model in the manner of *Rerum novarum*. However, they do present some general teachings that have served as a foundation for future social involvement by American Catholics.

In these two documents the bishops devoted considerable attention to the worker-employer relationship. While the bishops insisted that labor unions must be faithful to signed contracts with employers, their strongest language is reserved for the affirmation of the workers' basic right to organize, a right which may never again come into question.

The American bishops did display considerable optimism about this nation's ability and willingness to correct the specific abuses in its economic system which they roundly condemned in these two documents. No radical surgery was required in their judgment. Any thought of a turn towards a socialist model was definitely out of the question. But the bishops did take one step beyond merely asserting the basic right of union organizing. In the Program of Social Reconstruction they proposed a measure of worker copartnership in industrial decision-making and even the possibility of some form of worker ownership. A reflection of these themes continues in the 1986 pastoral, especially in the emphasis on worker *participation* which serves as a basic cornerstone of the bishops' letter. These were the actual words of the bishops in 1919: "The full possibilities of increased production will not be realized as long as the majority of the workers remain mere wage earners. The majority must somehow become owners, or at least in part, of the instruments of production. They can be enabled to reach this stage gradually through cooperative productive societies and copartnership arrangements" (#36).

The extreme economic difficulties which the nation faced during the Depression era resulted in the issuance of a number of major statements on the subject. The last of these in 1940 entitled Church and Social Order represented the most comprehensive attempt at an ethical analysis of the U.S. economy prior to the present pastoral.

A number of points in these five documents need to be highlighted. First of all, we notice that the earlier commitment of the bishops to union organizing and the just wage has in no way wavered. But in the interim some internal strife had arisen within the American labor movement and the bishops duly warned Catholics about being a party to such strife. They likewise reaffirmed their earlier rejection of all forms of Communist and Socialist economic theory, even the relatively mild proposals of Democratic Socialism. While the bishops had strong words for those versions of Capitalism that exaggerate individualism, they warned in their 1933 statement that "one of the greatest dangers facing us is a blind reaction from our former individualism to a regime of state socialism or state capitalism" (#73).

An overriding concern of the bishops in several of these documents was the growing concentration of wealth which engendered strong criticism from Pius XI in *Quadragesimo anno*. The bishops applied the papal warning to this country as they spoke of the many injustices resulting from the increased concentration of capital resources within American industry and the consequent control it gave to a small number of entrepreneurs. This was making widespread, meaningful participation in the economic system increasing difficult for most Americans. The 1940 episcopal statement confronted this situation without mincing any words: "The two great dangers which society faces in the present state of economic organization are, first, the concentration of ownership and control of wealth and, second, its anonymous character which results from some of the existing business and corporation law, whereby responsibility toward society is greatly impaired if not completely ignored" (#22).

The bishops did not confine themselves to critical analysis in these five documents. They offered as well the outlines of a solution. While once more reaffirming their staunch opposition to the socialist option, they insisted that government must play a significant mediating role in the American economy. The problems before the nation will not be solved, justice will not be enhanced, by the simple unrestrained dynamics of the market. The 1933 document Present Crisis insisted that a vital function of government is to "assist in the organization of the various economic groups" (#74). The 1940 declaration went even further in this regard: ". . . the civil authority . . . must so regulate the responsibility of property that the burden of providing for the common good be equitably distributed. It must furthermore establish such conditions through legal enactment and administration policy that wealth itself can be distributed so each individual member of society may surely and justly come into possession of the material goods necessary for his own livelihood" (#22).

This governmental role, the bishops went on to make clear, must always be conditioned by the traditional Catholic social principle of subsidiarity which insists on assigning a particular social function to the smallest effective unit. But contrary to what some have claimed in discussions about the present pastoral letter, the bishops of our day have not strayed totally from earlier episcopal pronouncements in their considerable emphasis on the role of government in solving the injustices inherent in the American economy. Rather, they have reaffirmed a notion of governmental activity as crucial for economic justice which had been firmly implanted in U.S. Catholic social teaching decades earlier. These documents likewise show that any claim that the proper definition of subsidiarity excludes significant, direct governmental intervention is indeed false.

During this crucial period of U.S. history the American Catholic leadership did not restrict itself merely to issuing statements on economic matters. Through the Bishops' Conference in Washington they took direct action in behalf of striking workers and endorsed federal legislation that would add to the dignity and security of the laboring class. Nearly all these activities took place in an interreligious context as leaders of Jewish organizations and the Protestant Federal Council of Churches joined with their Catholic counterparts in a manifestation of the best in the American spirit of religious pluralism. There was tri-faith involvement, for example, in the enginemen's strike on the Western Maryland Railroad in 1927 and in the investigation into the Armistice Day Tragedy of 1919 in Centralia, Washington in which worker lives were lost.

On the level of federal labor policy several important interventions were undertaken by representatives of the three faith
communities. December 1929 saw a joint Protestant-Catholic-
Jewish statement on conditions in the textile industry, followed
by one on unemployment in January 1932. The previous year
had seen tri-faith cosponsorship of a national conference on "Permanent Preventives of Unemployment" in Washington. And in
June 1932, when unemployment in the United States had risen
to alarming proportions and the federal government seemed
reluctant to take any decisive action to remedy the situation,
Rabi Edward L. Israel, Fr. R.A. McGowan and the Rev. James
Myers joined representatives of the American Federation of Labor and national farmers' organizations in testifying before the
House and Senate. In their presentations, broadcast on a nationwide radio hookup, they demanded an adequate response
to the unemployment crisis from government at both the federal
and local levels. Their testimony is credited with significant influence in bringing about congressional approval of the first federal funds for meeting this crisis later on that year.

Joint efforts continued in 1933. In July, after passage of the
National Industrial Recovery Act (NRA), the Central Conference
of American Rabbis and the Federal Council of Churches in con-
junction with the Catholic Bishops' Conference issued a public
statement outlining the social implications of this historic legislation. Signing for the Bishops' Conference was Msgr. John A.
Ryan. He is a figure whose achievements over a span of several
decades (1920–1945) as head of the Social Action Office of the
Bishops' Conference are too little known among American Catholics. Through his scholarly writings on ethics and economics
and his active involvement in the Washington political scene he
was tremendously influential in bringing about widespread support within the American hierarchy for the New Deal economic
reforms which did so much to upgrade the dignity of the working
class in this country. In many ways the 1986 pastoral letter is
part of the legacy that Msgr. Ryan helped to create over the
years.

Finally, in December 1933, representatives of the three major
faith communities appeared before the Committee of Ways and
Means of the House of Representatives, then in a discussion of

tax legislation, to offer interventions calling for laws that would ensure a more equitable distribution of wealth and income in the nation.

It is not possible, of course, to determine precisely the extent to which these tri-faith interventions impacted legislation in this country. But there is evidence they carried significant weight with legislators and opinion molders. Social researchers Claris Silcox and Galen Fisher of the Institute of Social and Religious Research in a study published in 1934 explicitly attributed the abolition of the twelve-hour day in the steel industry, for example, "in considerable measure" to these tri-faith efforts. Overall they concluded that "this close collaboration by these three agencies, speaking for tens of thousands of churches and synagogues, is considered by thoughtful men to have done much toward educating the conscience of the nation and toward demonstrating the courageous concern of all the creeds with justice and the good life . . . It has helped to disprove the charge that the religious bodies are class organizations, the tools and defenders of special interests." They go on to add that "the impartial array of facts and opinions undergirding most of the pronouncements has given the critics no ground to stand on, except the old assertion that the church should preach 'religion' and let economics alone." (*Catholics, Jews and Protestants: A Study of Relationships in the United States and Canada*, pp. 301–331)

The years following World War II brought new prosperity to the United States, especially to the working classes that included the majority of Catholics. The New Deal reforms and the successes of the unionization efforts, began to pay dividends. But new problems now faced the nation which the American bishops felt compelled to address.

Comprehensive, reflective statements on economic life came forth in 1953 and again in 1960. The former document highlighted several themes which have become a prominent part of Pope John Paul II's approach to economic issues (especially in the encyclical *Laborem exercens*) and which are crucial to the theological foundations of the present U.S. pastoral. One of these is the Incarnation. Another is the profound relationship between labor and human dignity. A third, related to the second, is the notion of human co-creational responsibility for the world. Human labor, the bishops said, enables people "to share in the creative work of God" (#30). The 1986 pastoral says much the same: "Men and women are also to share in the creative activity of God . . . They can justly consider that by their labor they are unfolding the Creator's work" (#32).

Both the 1953 and the 1960 statements emphasized liberty and the sense of personal responsibility as crucial ethical values in economic life. Both statements celebrated liberty and personal responsibility as central to the American experience in general and to our economic system in particular. Catholics committed to democratic Capitalism as the system most able to provide justice for the greatest number will certainly find strong support for their position in these two documents.

The civil rights movement of the sixties and the social activism triggered by the discovery of continuing widespread racism and poverty in America forced the bishops into a critical analysis of U.S. economic institutions. Without repudiating the American political ideal or the capitalist system at its heart, they were firm in maintaining that the nation could no longer ignore the cycle of poverty, often rooted in racism that so frequently engulfs the Black, Hispanic and Native American minorities in this land. What was done for the Catholic blue collar and mine workers through union organizing and the New Deal must now be done for these minorities. This is the clear challenge addressed in a special way to the new Catholic middle class in a 1966 document and one in 1970 launching the Campaign for Human Development. The latter argued forcefully that poverty can no longer be tolerated in America: "Poverty in the United States is a cruel anachronism today. At a time when most Americans enjoy unparalleled material bounty, it is unthinkable that some Americans should still be condemned to live out their lives within the 'hellish circle' of want. If we close our eyes to the continuing existence of poverty in our nation, we are vulnerable to the accusation of spiritual blindness and moral insensitivity." This document, influenced by Pope Paul VI's *Populorum progressio*, moved the church in America toward a realization of the need to remove sinful economic structures that lock the poor in a condition of ongoing dependency.

The final major document on economic matters prior to the present pastoral came out in 1975 in the midst of a severe recession. It was now becoming clear that not only the U.S. economy, but the world economy as well, had fallen into a deep malaise. This document offered some initial reflections on how Catholics might approach these continuing economic dilemmas. In so doing it serves as a direct prelude to the current pastoral. Among the points it stressed were economic sustainability as a right, the need to measure economic success primarily in terms of wealth distribution and not accumulation, the inherent right of every person to a job, the responsibility of government to provide employment when the private sector cannot do so, and the importance of broad participation in economic decisionmaking. All these principles are rooted in the teachings of Vatican II, John XXIII, and Paul VI. The bishops also turned their attention to the problem of inflation and its impact on the poor. Finally, they show sensitivity to the profound link between the distribution of wealth and social power: "The distribution of income and wealth are important since they influence and even determine our society's distribution of economic power. Catholic social teaching has condemned gross inequality in the distribution of material goods. Our country cannot continue to ignore this important measure of economic justice" (#18).

Even from this relatively cursory examination of the U.S. hierarchy's interventions in economic matters it should be evident that the 1986 pastoral does not represent a totally new departure by the bishops. Rather they have nearly a century of expressed concern for economic justice in America and the world, a concern that at key moments of American history involved not merely words but direct action. It is out of this rich legacy of word and deed that the present pastoral has emerged as the most comprehensive reflection to date.

FURTHER READINGS

Byers, David M., ed. *Justice in the Marketplace: Collected Statements of the Vatican and the U.S. Bishops on Economic Policy, 1891–1984,* with commentary by John T. Pawlikowski, O.S.M. Washington, D.C.: United States Catholic Conference, 1985.

Coleman, John. *An American Strategic Theology.* New York: Paulist Press, 1982. (pp. 85–97, on Msgr. John A. Ryan)

Curran, Charles. *American Catholic Social Ethics: Twentieth Century Approaches.* Notre Dame: University of Notre Dame Press, 1982. (pp. 26–91, on Msgr. John A. Ryan)

Grelle, Bruce and David A. Krueger, eds. *Christianity and Capitalism. Perspectives on Religion, Liberalism and the Economy.* Chicago: Center for the Scientific Study of Religion, 1986.

Higgins, George G. "Religion and Economic Policy: A Catholic Perspective." In *Formation of Social Policy in the Catholic and Jewish Traditions*, edited by Eugene J. Fisher and Daniel F. Polish. Notre Dame: University of Notre Dame Press, 1980.

QUESTIONS

1. What are some of the basic implications of the notion of human co-creatorship for an American Christian's participation in economic life?

2. How do you understand "structural sin" in the economic sphere? What are some examples within the U.S. economic system?

3. Do you believe that the record of the American bishops on economic questions throughout this century shows a decided "preferential option for the poor"?

4. What are the key elements of a just economic system as outlined in the documents issued by the American bishops from 1919 through the present pastoral? Do you detect evolution in any areas?

6

The Church's Common Moral Vision and the Vision of the Economic Pastoral

Thomas Nairn, O.F.M.

THE STATED PURPOSE OF THE PASTORAL LETTER *ECONOMIC JUSTICE for All* is actually a dual one, for the bishops to "add [the church's] voice to the public debate about the directions in which the U.S. economy should be moving" (#27) and for them to help Catholics "as they seek to form their consciences about economic matters" (#27).

This dual emphasis, effectively used in the 1983 peace pastoral, continues to serve the bishops well. For those outside the church, the bishops use the notions of common good and the language of human rights to describe the minimum conditions they consider are needed for social institutions to respect human dignity, social solidarity, and justice (#79ff.). For those inside the church, the letter develops a similar argument, based upon Scripture and church tradition, that concludes in listing several moral priorities in the area of economics which follow from our Catholic faith.

Thus, although the letter speaks about current American economic policy, it is not primarily an economic or political document. It is most basically a statement of faith, stemming from a community of faith. The bishops speak of a common moral vision found in our tradition (#23), a vision and tradition which are "dynamic and growing" (#26). In the questions it asks, in the

49

answers it attempts, in both its content and its form, the bishops' pastoral letter is a Roman Catholic faith document arising from our tradition and carrying this tradition forward as the bishops interact with the issues facing our contemporary American culture.

The Catholic Social Tradition

Thus the pastoral stems from that common moral vision which itself sustains Christianity (#22ff.). Concern for the poor has indeed been part of this moral vision or attitude from the church's earliest days. For example, sometime around 125A.D., the Greek philosopher Aristides described what impressed him about the new Christian community in these words: "If there is among them anyone who is poor and in need, and they do not have an abundance of necessities, they fast two or three days, that they may supply the needy with their necessary food." That element which spoke most eloquently about the Christian faith was the care which Christians showed to one another and especially to the poor.

As centuries progressed, members of the church continued serious moral reflection on this vision. The pastoral briefly describes this history (#56–60). From St. Ambrose and St. Thomas Aquinas through Pope Leo XIII to Pope John Paul II, the church has responded to problems facing society. As the pastoral itself notes, "throughout its history, the Christian community has listened to the words of Scripture and sought to enact them in the midst of daily life in very different historical and cultural contexts" (#56). This history, which the bishops call "a living, growing resource that can inspire hope and help shape the future" (#26), is filled with decisive moments when the church had to ask anew how our living faith was able to show itself concretely in works of justice and love.

One such important turning point occurred in 1891 with the promulgation of Pope Leo XIII's encyclical, "On the Condition of the Working Class" (*Rerum novarum*). The Latin title is translated as "of new things." The church was definitely speaking about new things but did so by looking at its own past. Although he based his thought on the centuries-old notion of a natural order of society determined by God, Pope Leo issued his letter as a protest against the current exploitation of poor workers. In doing so, he laid a foundation upon which future church documents would build. Possibly even more significant than what the encyclical said was the very fact that the church could not be silent about injustice. In speaking out, Pope Leo articulated anew and developed that common moral vision, a vision further enhanced by the works of Popes Pius XI and XII.

The immigrants to this country in the early part of this century were the special beneficiaries of these writings. Catholics became prominent in the struggle for just wages, decent working conditions and hours, the right to unionize, and the right for all to participate in our country's political processes.

The brief pontificate of John XXIII witnessed even further changes in the church's understanding of its social task. Both of his major encyclicals, Christianity and Social Progress (*Mater et magistra*, May 15, 1961) and Peace on Earth (*Pacem in terris*, April 11, 1963), speak of the dignity of the person as created in the image of God. They use this understanding as the theological basis for the church's reflection upon the tradition of human rights.

Pope John also provided new tools to help the church in its social task. Chief among these was his analysis of the "signs of the times" as testimonies of God's activity in the world: advances of the working class, women in public life, greater consciousness of human dignity, developing countries achieving independence, arms negotiations. Pope John saw these events in the world as witnesses of God's providential care.

This new direction, begun by Pope John, continued in the Second Vatican Council, especially in Pastoral Constitution on the Church in the Modern World. Attempting to address the "particularly urgent needs characterizing the present age," the Council returned to Pope John's reading of the "signs of the times." The Council emphasized that the human person is an historical being in the world. Therefore, having a history is part of what it means to be human. Once Christians acknowledge history, however, we must see ourselves as called to analyze the changes around us and see how these changes affect other human beings, all images of our God, all sisters and brothers. Secular events thus have an importance for the church, even if they do nothing more than raise the questions which Christians must try to answer. The times themselves have something to teach us in the church.

In taking human society (the world) seriously, the Council was able to pose questions absent prior to that time. It was able to take seriously the Gospel and that common Christian moral vision which judge and challenge all of us. It was also able to take seriously concrete human experience. The Council however saw a world which not only witnessed God's providential care but which also was a place where injustice occurred and which was itself longing for redemption.

Gospel and human experience tell us that indeed injustice exists in our present world and that this injustice actually threatens the future of our world. What the Gospel does not provide us with, however, is a detailed blueprint to lead us easily from our present state to that sort of world which the Gospel demands. The Council insisted time and time again that the church does not have all the solutions to the world's needs, but it also emphasized that it did have something to contribute towards a solution. It asked all members of the church to take up the task of working for a more just world and for the development of all people. The Second Synod of Bishops, meeting in Rome in 1971, continued scrutinizing the "signs of the times" and concluded that "action on behalf of justice and participation in the transformation of the world" was "a constitutive dimension of the preaching of the Gospel."

The time from Pope Leo XIII to today witnessed another development, more subtle but equally important. The world addressed by the church has grown since the days of Pope Leo. The exploited workers who were the focus of his encyclical lived in Western Europe and North America. Pope Pius XII and especially Pope John XIII had to acknowledge the importance to the church of the part of the world which lived under the influence of the Soviet Union. Signed copies of Pope John's encyclical Peace on Earth were delivered both to President Kennedy and to Premier Khrushchev. The Second Vatican Council's Pastoral Constitution on the Church in the Modern World owes its existence in a significant way to the bishops from Latin America, Africa, Asia, and Oceania. These third world Catholics have had an increasingly important role to play in the church since the Council. The Catholic Church is not a European church or even a church of the northern hemisphere but a global church.

Membership in such a global community challenges all members of the church. No longer is one able to look merely to one's own country or even hemisphere in attempting to address the questions of the common good. The U.S. bishops are correct in speaking of the "moral responsibility of citizens to serve the common good of the entire planet" (#322). This expansion of our church's vision implies that the suffering and injustice which occur in Latin America or Africa or Asia must have an effect on the church in North America or Europe. Catholics must be concerned about what is happening in the entire world.

The church's recent history seems to call us back to the description of the Christian community which began this section. Christians of all times have been responsible for helping the poor in their midst. In the early decades of the church, it could respond by the community calling a fast. Today, churchgoers contributing to the Bishops' Campaign for Human Development, Catholics working in soup kitchens or in food pantries or in shelters for the homeless, people exercising their constitutional right of writing letters and petitioning their legislators on issues affecting the poor in America and throughout the world, bishops writing a letter on the American economy are all contributing to making the vision expressed in the Council, that moral vision evidenced in many different ways throughout our history, a reality in our country at the present time. The task of the church cannot be separated from these concrete acts of justice.

"Economic Justice for All"

The bishops' pastoral is a call to the U.S. Catholic community to carry on this social tradition of our church and to embody it in our lives by working for justice and by an active love of neighbor (#60). In issuing this call, they again make explicit our tradition's common moral vision, further developing it against the economic questions which are especially urgent today.

At the basis of this common vision is the dignity of the person created in the very image of God and called to share in God's creative activity (#32). Human dignity was the reason for Pope Leo's protest against the exploitation of workers in his day and behind Pope John's articulation of human rights. Likewise, the bishops maintain that "the dignity of the human person, realized in community with others, is the criterion against which all aspects of economic life must be measured" (#28). Every element of the pastoral returns to this basic belief.

For us in the U.S. today, such dignity seems to demand that

all persons actively participate in our country's economic process. The pastoral itself begins with three now famous questions: "What does the economy do *for* people? What does it do *to* people? And how do people *participate* in it?" Answering these questions leads those in the church to engage in those sorts of actions which allow people to contribute to society in ways which respect their freedom and dignity (#72) and which seek to overcome marginalization and powerlessness (#77). The pastoral calls this sort of activity the most basic demand of justice (#78). Catholics must not only be active in our country's economic life, but as Catholics we are to make that life more just, more equitable, and more participative, confronting those elements in our society which threaten such participation.

The letter further calls U.S. Catholics to become more genuinely concerned not only about participation in our nation's economy but also about the planetary common good. The bishops maintain:

> Nations separated by geography, culture and ideology are linked in a complex commercial, financial, technological and environmental network. These links have two direct consequences. First, they create hope for a new form of community among all peoples, one built on dignity, solidarity and justice. Second, this rising global awareness calls for greater attention to the stark inequities across countries in the standard of living and control of resources (#13).

As members of a global church, we are urged to work to make this new form of community a reality both in our nation and in the entire world.

The pastoral then is actually calling us to conversion. The bishops ask all Catholics to examine our way of living in light of the needs of the poor (#75). As in the early church, we are called to fast, to cut back on what we do not need so that we may supply the needy of the world with necessities. But we are also called to a living faith which bears fruit in the way society is structured: "The transformation of social structures begins with and is always accompanied by a conversion of heart" (#328). The most powerful lesson the church can give the world is the example of the lives of its members. Thus the pastoral ends with an urgent call to holiness on the part of its members, acknowledging that the church must become the model for society of collaboration and participation (#358) and must renew itself as regards its own economic life (#349).

A major question which remains before us in the church is whether we will accept this social dimension of the process of conversion. Bishop James Malone, former president of the National Conference of Catholic Bishops, has noted that unlike the immigrants in the United States at the beginning of this century, many Catholics today are no longer the beneficiaries of the church's social teaching. He then asked the troubling question whether, since we no longer benefit, are we any longer interested in that teaching? At the core of his question is whether or not we continue to accept that common moral vision enunciated throughout our history.

It is indeed a troubling question, but one which Catholics have faced in the past and must continually face. We can only answer the question from our own center of faith. Perhaps that is why the bishops conclude the pastoral with their act of faith in that God which inspires our common moral vision and whose Spirit carries that vision forward:

> We must not be discouraged. In the midst of this struggle it is inevitable that we become aware of greed, laziness and envy. No utopia is possible on this earth; but as believers in the redemptive love of God and as those who have experienced God's forgiving mercy, we know that God's providence is not and will not be lacking to us today (#364).

The pastoral is a statement of faith, the product here and now of a common moral vision which has nourished our church throughout its history. As such it deserves to be taken seriously by all men and women of faith.

FURTHER READINGS

Byers, David, ed. *Justice in the Marketplace: Collected Statements of the Vatican and the U.S. Catholic Bishops on Economic Policy, 1891–1984.* Washington, D.C.: United States Catholic Conference, 1985.

Dorr, Donal. *Option for the Poor: A Hundred Years of Vatican Social Teaching.* Maryknoll, N.Y.: Orbis Books, 1983.

QUESTIONS

1. Do we Catholics know the social tradition of the church as well as we know its stands on more personal moral issues?

2. Ought the lives and struggles of Catholics living in Latin America, Asia, or Africa affect the church in the United States?

3. How would you answer Bishop Malone's question?

4. How central ought the question of justice be in the church's teaching? In parish life? In your own Christian life?

5. How can we embody this "common moral vision" of our tradition in our daily lives?

7

The Common Good: Why There Can Be No Justice Without It

Paul J. Wadell, C.P.

CATHOLIC SOCIAL TEACHING HAS ALWAYS MADE SOME CURIOUS claims, but one of the most curious is that ultimately personal good and common good are one. This is strange music to anyone accustomed to think of the common good not enabling individual good but restricting it, and very strange music to anyone who thinks justice works not to achieve the common good, but to establish the conditions in which all of us can pursue what we desire with minimum hindrance from others. That is how many of us have been tutored to think of justice, but it is just such thinking that finally makes justice impossible. There can be no justice without the common good, for the common good is what genuine justice always seeks.

This is the insight empowering *Economic Justice for All*, the pastoral letter on Catholic social teaching and the U.S. economy recently issued by the National Conference on Catholic Bishops. The common good is a theme, an organizing principle, threaded throughout the letter. From first to last it is the vision from which the letter is born and the goal it seeks to effect. In the opening paragraphs of the pastoral, which are something of an overture cluing us in on the tone and direction of the letter, the bishops make clear that every perspective on the economy, particularly its moral perspective, must be evaluated in light of the common good. And near the end of their letter, the bishops insist it is only a commitment to the common good that makes a just economy possible (#331).

But they are also alarmed. They know there cannot be justice without the common good, but it is exactly an understanding of and commitment to the common good they fear is missing in our country today. Signs of its absence are everywhere. As the bishops survey the American landscape what do they see? They see a widening gulf between the rich and the poor. They see grievously unacceptable levels of unemployment and poverty. They see too much money spent on defense and not enough money spent to create jobs. They see a culture dangerously inclined to the idolatry of wealth, a culture that too often emphasizes "values and aims that are selfish, wasteful and opposed to the Scriptures" (#334). As they look across the American landscape, they see a society that is fragmented and a people whose isolation and loneliness is a direct reflection of the justice they lack.

The way to justice is through the common good. The bishops know this and that is why the brunt of the pastoral is a call to rediscover it. The bishops speak of this in various ways. They call for a "new American Experiment" to create an order "that guarantees the minimum conditions of human dignity in the economic sphere for every person" (#95). They challenge us to "an imaginative vision of the future that can help shape economic arrangements in creative new ways" (#295), and they remind us that "only new forms of cooperation and partnership" (#296) make justice possible. But the point is always the same: "Only a renewed commitment by all to the common good can deal creatively with the realities of international interdependence and economic dislocations in the domestic economy" (#296). Only through the common good can injustice be overcome.

The Common Good: Why Its Meaning Must Be Taken from God

If justice hinges on the common good, it matters much how we understand it. In the Catholic social tradition, the common good was never the sum of individuals' good; rather, the common good was justice working to achieve the highest and most proper human good; it was justice working to achieve the optimum development of humanity, and for Christians that is the union of all people with God. As the bishops note, "Vatican II described the common good as 'the sum of those conditions of social life which allow social groups and their individual members relatively thorough and ready access to their own fulfillment,'" (#79) and in the Christian vision of faith the fulfillment of every person involves "communion with God, sharing God's life," and "a mutual bonding with all on this globe" (#364).

In the Catholic social tradition, the substance of the common good is taken from humanity's grandest possibility. This means the common good is defined not in itself, but in terms of the singlemost indispensable good on which human life ultimately depends. To know the common good we must ask for what is human life given? For Christians it is community of life with all humanity in God. God who is our ultimate and most perfect good is truly the only genuine common good for it is through seeking and being united to God that all of us most fully are.

In the Catholic social tradition, the common good is focused on God who stands as the end and ultimate perfection of life. We read the world not in its own light, but in light of the God we are called to resemble; we understand our life in the world, what it can be and is meant to be, from the Kingdom we should make our own. To make God the common good is to recognize how everything in society, including the economy, must tend to and enable the liberation of all in God. If justice works to achieve the common good, then in the Christian vision justice is organizing society in such a way that all of us and our world reach God. In other words, if God is the common good, justice works to bring about the Kingdom. What our world should be, how we should understand it, how we should be in it, depends on who we ultimately should be. In Catholic social ethics, the form society should take now is determined by the society all of us are called to be when we are gathered together in the lovelife of God. The Kingdom is a society, too, the society of perfect friendship, of mutual delight and adoration in God, and even though the Kingdom cannot be perfectly reached in this world, it is the Kingdom that tells us what our world should be.

To read the world in light of God is the beginning of justice for it is to see clearly the common good for which every other good exists. Far from diminishing the value of created goods, seeing them serving and enabling Kingdom justice is the only understanding of them that is not idolatrous. Material things are not bad, but our love for them can be. As Jean Mouroux says so well, "in the hands of a rightful love," a love that seeks God most of all, the goods of the earth are means of gaining God, they are instruments to reunion. The value of all these things is that they are gifts from God to serve us in establishing the justice which empowers Kingdom life. (*The Meaning of Man*, pp.25–27) If we love God most of all, we know how to love rightly everything else, that is the insight forming the Christian understanding of the common good. Once God is seen to be the one unsurpassable good, every other good is seen for what it truly and gracefully is: a gift from God which enables reunion with God. As Jacques Maritain puts it, "Everything else—the whole universe and every social institution—must ultimately minister to this purpose; everything must foster and strengthen and protect the conversation of the soul, every soul, with God." (*The Person and the Common Good*, p.16)

That is why the signs of injustice the bishops spot in our country today persist not because the economy is complex and our industries are changing, but because our loves remain disordered. Ultimately, unemployment, poverty, the ravaged lives of minorities never allowed fully to belong, witness not what must be in a less than perfect world, but what will always be if our loves remain false. That "28 percent of the total net wealth is held by the richest 2 percent of families in the United States" (#183) argues not that there must be gross inequality to make the economy work, not even that there must be gross inequality in a fallen, sinful world; no, it simply reminds us that the common good is forgotten not because it is impractical, but because it is a threat to the idolatry of wealth, an idolatry that ravages not only the poor who are denied the goods they deserve, but also the wealthy who unknowingly become as false as their loves. Created goods are not dangerous, but people of misdirected loves are. They are dangerous to others because of the justice they deny them, and dangerous to themselves because of what their loves make them. The ultimate effect of false loves is oblivion, a perduring forgetfulness of who we are called to be by God. It is exactly this the Christian sense of the common good helps us remember.

The Common Good: What It Tells Us About Ourselves

There is a scene in John Steinbeck's great novel, *The Grapes of Wrath*, where the onetime huckster preacher, Jim Casy, undergoes a conversion. Like the Jesus he claimed to follow, Jim goes out to the wilderness to try to understand the world. It is there that he has an insight that turns his life around. As he explains to his friend, Tom Joad,

> "An' I got thinkin', on'y it wasn't thinkin', it was deeper down than thinkin'. I got thinkin' how we was holy when we was one thing, an' mankin' was holy when it was one thing. An' it on'y got unholy when one mis'able little fella got the bit in his teeth an' run off his own way, kickin' an' draggin' an' fightin'. Fella like that bust the holiness. But when they're all workin' together, not one fella for another fella, but one fella kind of harnessed to the whole shebang—that's right, that's holy." (*Grapes of Wrath*, p.88)

If the common good is rooted in an understanding of God, it also fosters a special understanding of ourselves. What Jim Casy was thinking about in the desert that day is something all of us should consider. When he realized "we was holy when we was one thing," Jim had an insight into the Mystical Body, he realized the essential solidarity of the human race. The bishops are straightforward about this. "Human life is life in community," they tell us, and "Christians look forward in hope to a true communion among all persons with each other and with God. The Spirit of Christ labors in history to build up the bonds of solidarity among all persons until that day on which their union is brought to perfection in the kingdom of God" (#63–64).

We are all members one of another, that is what the common good attests and that is why it does not oppose personal good but enables it. The common good is the condition of personal good because none of us can flourish, none of us can have life at all, unless we have it in common, unless it is shared, mutual, reciprocal life, unless it is life not hindering but leading to com-munion. As the bishops write, "These insights show that human beings achieve self-realization not in isolation, but in interaction with others" (#65), and that is why justice, the virtue which orders our relationships with others, is also the virtue which enables us to be a self. Human life is relational, and that means not only that selfhood requires others, but more precisely that being a self is abiding in relationship with others.

Human existence is not solitary, it is participated. As God's very life in the Trinity tells us, our life is not and cannot be self-constituted, it is other-constituted. For us to be is to be communally, and for us to be wholly is to be marked by the same generosity and communion that marks God. What Maritain says about the life of God can also, analogously, be said about ourselves: "Each one is in the other through an infinite communion, the common good of which is strictly and absolutely the proper good of each." (*The Person and the Common Good*, p.58) We experience this truth about ourselves in all those redemptive moments in which we realize how our growth and development, indeed the possibility of being a self at all, depends on our capacity to overcome selfishness, depends on our capacity to move from self-absorption to communion, from grasping our life to sharing it.

The common good both rests on and enables this understanding of the self. But perhaps it also explains why living in a country as wealthy and blessed as ours can also leave us so lonely: we forget the community each of us is. As Dorothy Day mused in her poignant autobiography, *The Long Loneliness*, life always takes the form of the long loneliness anytime we deny the kinship we have with one another. Dorothy Day did not deny loneliness will be a part of any pilgrimage life, but she was convinced we are often lonelier than we need to be because we fear admitting the kinship we have with all children of God. Dorothy Day saw that the long loneliness we feel in our hearts is not so much the human condition as it is the effect of injustice, the effect of being out of relationship with those without whom we cannot be at all. We are lonely because we deny the community we are and fear how such community might change us. Still, the longer we deny that community the more impoverished and stunted we remain for we never come into touch with the others who give us life. As Dorothy Day explained, "The only answer in this life, to the loneliness we are all bound to feel, is community." (*The Long Loneliness*, p.272)

The Common Good and the Conversion That Makes It Possible

The common good requires seeing our world and ourselves a certain way, but it is not a seeing we naturally achieve. A commitment to the common good is necessary for a just society, but conversion is necessary for that. There is simply too much in ourselves and in our society that works against the common good. There is selfishness and greed and fear in ourselves, and we have social structures which reflect that. There is a penchant in ourselves to materialism, the temptation to think that existence is secured not through other people but through things. As Steinbeck puts it, "For the quality of owning freezes you forever into 'I,' and cuts you off forever from the 'we.' " (*Grapes of Wrath*, p.166)

If we are not to be "cut off forever from the 'we,' " we have to be willing to change. In order to sustain the common good, we have to be willing to become good ourselves. The bishops admit this. All their talk about a just social order remains chimerical unless we are willing to become a just people. A just society begins in our conversion to justice. As they explain, "The transformation of social structures begins with and is always accompanied by a conversion of the heart," and practically that demands the "personal struggle to control greed and selfishness, a personal commitment to reverence one's own human dignity and the dignity of others by avoiding self-indulgence and those attachments that make us insensitive to the conditions of others and that erode social solidarity" (#328).

As the bishops' words make clear, a conversion to the common good begins in a conversion in ourself, the deliberate, painstaking transformation of self by which our desires, loves, cares and concerns are purified of the dross of selfishness and graced with the generosity and compassion of Christ. It begins when we no longer fear Kingdom justice, but actually embody it.

Further Readings

Bellah, Robert N., et al. *Habits of the Heart*. Berkeley: University of California Press, 1985.

Day, Dorothy. *The Long Loneliness*. New York: Curtis Books, 1952.

Haughey, John C., ed., *The Faith That Does Justice*. New York: Paulist Press, 1977.

Maritain, Jacques. *The Person and the Common Good*. Notre Dame: University of Notre Dame Press, 1966.

Questions

1. What do you think most Americans understand the common good to be? How would they explain it?

2. Why is justice impossible without a commitment to the common good?

3. What in our country today are some common impediments to realizing the common good?

4. Is there anything Christians and the church can do to foster a deeper appreciation of the common good?

8

Economic Rights and the Principle of Subsidiarity

John Paul Szura, O.S.A.

HUMAN BEINGS HAVE ECONOMIC RIGHTS. HUMAN BEINGS NEED OTH-ers in order to develop fully. These two teachings are at the heart of a Gospel vision proposed by the U.S. bishops in their 1986 economic pastoral letter. This letter, *Economic Justice for All*, applies traditional Catholic social teaching to the situation in the United States. The bishops call for a "new American experiment." They call for conversion and action. They call their church not to a new doctrine but a renewed challenge to bring economic justice to all. And they present this challenge as a Gospel vision in which each person supports the economic rights of all by the help that comes only from solidarity with others.

The U.S. bishops write at a time when the entire church is more aware of the hunger within people both to live fully as persons and to live with others. It is also a time when economic injustices violate personal dignity and when social injustices keep many from solidarity with others. This pastoral letter is thus a prophetic call to recognize the signs of the times, which now more clearly demand that economic justice flow from personal growth supported by others. And the name given to the Gospel law that our personhood grow with proper support from others is the "principle of subsidiarity."

This pastoral letter is coming at a critical time for our nation and world. Economic problems abound, and the numbers of poor, hungry, and homeless are increasing. Lack of proper work is a scandal. In this crisis people are more loudly demanding personal dignity and solidarity. These demands mean that the church must return to the Gospel foundations of her social teaching. Because a cornerstone of this foundation is the principle of subsidiarity, we as church must make this principle a living force. Subsidiarity must become a vital element of our social teaching and of our spirituality as well.

The following reflections are offered in the hope that the U.S. economic pastoral letter may be the occasion for a renewal deep within us of the traditional principle of subsidiarity. We will look briefly at the recent development of that principle and how this development comes together in the pastoral letter. This short space will allow only a few indications of the richness of that principle. But that may be enough to show how it should penetrate our lives.

Principle of Subsidiarity: Its Recent Development

Our English word "subsidiarity" comes from the Latin word *subsidium* and means "help". It refers to the profound drive in human beings to seek from others the help needed to become or do something. This drive is at the root of groups—professional associations, unions, communities, friendships, families, governments, churches. The human person naturally seeks bonds and links with others in order to be effective, happy, truly human, and even to survive. Though membership in a particular group may be voluntary, people must in some way join with others. The human person cries out for a fulfillment it cannot attain in solitude or isolation.

Getting needed help from others is not opposed to personal growth. You are not less a person just because you could not be or do something all alone. But help that is not needed is another matter. Dependence upon others for what you can do yourself does not promote personal growth. This dependence leads to loss of identity and to absorption into another. You are not being helped but being smothered. The classical formulation of the principle of subsidiarity that describes needed help is found in

Pope Pius XI's 1931 social encyclical *Quadragesimo anno:*

> Just as it is gravely wrong to take from individuals what they can accomplish by their own initiative and industry and give it to the community, so also it is an injustice and at the same time a grave evil and disturbance of right order to assign to a greater and higher association what lesser and subordinate organizations can do. For every social activity ought of its very nature to furnish help to the members of the body social, and never destroy and absorb them. (#79)

Though Pius XI wrote its classical formulation in 1931, the principle of subsidiarity predated him by far. In 1891 Pope Leo XIII's great social encyclical *Rerum novarum* warned against the state absorbing individuals or families (#35) but also noted how natural it was to bond together for needed help (#50, 51). But Pope Leo was only bearing witness to Scripture and perennial Catholic social thought: the human person needs others for a help that does not smother or destroy.

Pope Pius XI formulated the principle of subsidiarity accenting personal initiative and creativity. He emphasized the danger of being smothered with help that was not really needed. As the world became more complicated and as injustices and economic imbalances grew more intolerable, people and families simply needed more help. Thus Pope John XXIII in his 1961 social encyclical *Mater et magistra* developed the classical formulation of Pius XI:

> At the outset it should be affirmed that in economic affairs first place is to be given to the private initiative of individual men who, either working by themselves, or with others in one fashion or another, pursue their common interests. (#51)

> But in this matter, for reasons pointed out by our predecessors, it is necessary that public authority take active interest, the better to increase output of goods and to further social progress for the benefit of all citizens. (#52)

> This intervention of public authorities that encourages, stimulates, regulates, supplements, and complements, is based on the principle of subsidiarity as set forth by Pius XI in his encyclical *Quadragesimo anno.* (#53)

Pope John was severely criticized by right wing authors because he understood the principle of subsidiarity as a basis for government intervention on behalf of those who need help. Nevertheless this was a legitimate development. Pope John did not take away initiative or creativity from persons or small groups. He simply recognized that subsidiarity means help and help is often badly needed. Further developments were to come.

In 1963 Pope John XXIII wrote his encyclical on peace, *Pacem in terris*. He linked peace with human rights and included economic rights among them (#11–22). These are the right to work, to a proper wage and healthy workplace, to private property, and to carry on economic activities. People have a fundamental right to life and to all that is necessary for life and bodily wholeness: food, clothing, shelter, rest, medical care, social services, and security in case of sickness or unemployment. Furthermore, public authority is responsible for promoting the common good by providing a climate in which human rights can thrive (#60–66). This responsibility of the state is based upon the principle of subsidiarity:

> The common good requires that civil authorities maintain a careful balance between coordinating and protecting the rights of the citizens, on the one hand, and promoting them, on the other . . . Nor should it happen that governments, in seeking to protect these rights, become obstacles to their full expression and free use.

> For this principle must always be retained: that state activity in the economic field, no matter what its breadth or depth may be, ought not to be exercised in such a way as to curtail an individual's freedom of personal initiative. Rather it should work to expand that freedom as much as possible by the effective protection of the essential personal rights of each and every individual. (#65)

The popes did not unfold or expand the principle of subsidiarity by adding new elements from the outside. They rather shifted emphasis or accent from one already present element to another. Church formulations of this principle always at least implicitly contained fear of absorption by a higher group and need for intervention from above; care for the common good and recognition of individual economic rights; respect for personal creative initiative and seeking help from others. The principle of subsidiarity grew because of human dignity's growing demands within increasingly complex world situations. These demands were heard by the Second Vatican Council, which understood the principle of subsidiarity in the context of human activity.

The great social document of the Second Vatican Council was *Gaudium et spes* (Church in the Modern World), and key to its vision was human activity. The first three chapters of *Gaudium et spes* tightly interrelate human activity, personal dignity, and solidarity with others. Later chapters treat human rights, justice, and peace. The principle of subsidiarity now clearly demands that society promote and protect human rights—including economic rights—by promoting and protecting human activity, personal dignity, and solidarity with others.

The human family and its individual members must actively and in solidarity participate in their own development and that of the world, helped by groups and governments. It is this developed understanding of the principle of subsidiarity that underlies the social teaching of the U.S. bishops.

Principle of Subsidiarity: the U.S. Economic Pastoral Letter

The U.S. bishops quote in their letter Pope Pius XI's classical formulation of the principle of subsidiarity (#99). But they also comment:

> This principle guarantees institutional pluralism. It provides space for freedom, initiative and creativity on the part of many social agents. At the same time, it insists that all these agents should work in ways that help build up the social body. Therefore, in all their activities these groups should be working in ways that express their distinctive capacities for action, that help meet human needs, and that make true contributions to the common good of the human community (#100).

Thus the U.S. bishops understand subsidiarity precisely as it has developed recently in Catholic thought. They give scope to person and take care that individuals are not absorbed by governments or groups. They demand that people be given needed help. Their mention of "common good" links subsidiarity to economic rights, for they previously defined common good in terms of those rights (#79, 80). And they see subsidiarity as a call to promote human activity, for they refer their comments in #100 to that section of *Gaudium et spes* encouraging responsibility and participation (#31).

But the pastoral letter does not merely teach the principle of subsidiarity in one section. This principle imbues its entirety, giving it a tone and context. This is evident from those parts of the letter which reveal the heart of its teaching:

First, the bishops list in a Pastoral Message the six principal themes of their letter. These are essentially the issues around which the principle of subsidiarity has been developed in recent Catholic thought:

> Every economic decision and institution must be judged in light of whether it protects or undermines the dignity of the human person. (#13)

> Human dignity can be realized and protected only in community. (#14)

> All people have a right to participate in the economic life of society. (#15)

> All members of society have a special obligation to the poor and vulnerable . . . This "option for the poor" does not mean pitting one group against another, but rather, strengthening the whole community by assisting those who are most vulnerable. (#16)

> Human rights are the minimum conditions for life in community. In Catholic teaching, human rights include not only civil and political rights but also economic rights. (#17)

> Society as a whole, acting through public and private institutions, has the moral responsibility to enhance human dignity and protect human rights. (#18)

Second, at the beginning of the letter the bishops orient their teaching toward human activity and help:

> Every perspective on economic life that is human, moral, and Christian must be shaped by three questions: What does the econ-

omy do for people? What does it do to people? And how do people participate in it? (#1)

3 Third, their fundamental moral and biblical vision embraces personal dignity fulfilled by helping communities:

> The basis for all that the Church believes about the moral dimensions of economic life is its vision of the transcendent worth—the sacredness—of human beings. The dignity of the human person, realized in community with others, is the criterion against which all aspects of economic life must be measured . . . all economic institutions must support the bonds of community and solidarity that are essential to the dignity of persons. (#28)

> As such every human being possesses an inalienable dignity that stamps human existence prior to any division into races or nations and prior to human labor and human achievement. Men and women are also to share in the creative activity of God. (#32)

> The same God who came to the aid of an oppressed people and formed them into a covenant community continues to hear the cries of the oppressed and to create communities which are responsive to God's word. (#40)

Finally, the bishops' policy suggestions aim at empowering human activity. "Full employment is the foundation of a just economy" (#136). "Employment is a basic right, a right which protects the freedom of all to participate in the economic life of society" (#137). "We recommend that the nation make a major new commitment to achieve full employment" (#151). "The most appropriate and fundamental solutions to poverty will be those that enable people to take control of their own lives (#188).

What is clear from this glance at the letter is confirmed by reading its entirety: it is penetrated by the principle of subsidiarity. But this is to say that the letter is penetrated by the spirit of Christ. For by now it should be clear we were not merely exploring a principle. We were exploring vital structures of human life, what the early church called "the footprints of the Trinity." We were reflecting upon Christian love. We were reflecting upon Christ, who became poor that we might share his riches.

Further Readings

Cardenal, Ernesto. *The Gospel in Solentiname.* Maryknoll, N.Y.: Orbis Books.

Day, Dorothy. *The Long Loneliness: An Autobiography.* San Francisco: Harper & Row, 1952.

Geremillion, Joseph, ed. *The Gospel of Peace and Justice.* Maryknoll, N.Y.: Orbis Books, 1976.

John Paul II, Pope. *Laborem exercens* (On Human Work).

Sinclair, Upton. *Jungle.* New York: Bantam Books, 1981.

Questions

1. If the principle of subsidiarity were followed according to the understanding of the church, what would health care delivery be like in our nation? Food distribution? Shelter?

2. One way the economic pastoral letter expresses the principle of subsidiarity is to reject the claim that "the government that governs least governs best" (#124). What direction should our government take in order to govern best?

3. Some people claim that capitalism promotes freedom and political rights, while socialism promotes equality and economic rights. How can we promote both freedom and equality? Political and economic rights?

4. The principle of subsidiarity is vital for Catholics seeking social and economic justice. Can it be just as vital for Catholics in their lives as parish members? People of prayer and reflection? Members of a world church?

THE PASTORAL PERSPECTIVE

9

Love, Justice, and Mutuality: The Foundations of Transformation

Marie McCarthy, S.P.

IN THE EARLY 1970S THERE WAS A GAME POPULAR AMONG BUSINESS and church groups involved in training people in leadership and group process skills. It was a monopoly style game in which participants were told that their goal was to "Win as much as you can." What participants were not told was that the more they cooperated with every other player in the game the more they themselves would win. The secret of the game was that no one could win unless everyone won. That game provides a helpful metaphor for exploring the spiritual and psychological dynamics involved in bringing about the vision presented in the U.S. Catholic bishops' pastoral letter, *Economic Justice for All*.

The Scope and Intent of the Pastoral

This pastoral letter has a threefold purpose. In the first instance it provides a powerful statement of the ideal toward which the Gospel message calls us, an ideal grounded in the command to love God and neighbor. That love command, which forms the heart of the Christian tradition, affirms the fundamental, unassailable dignity of every human being and calls us to strive toward the establishing of the reign of God here and now, a reign characterized by participation, mutuality, and community.

In the second instance the pastoral letter calls us to examine the concrete circumstances of this historical, cultural moment in light of that command to love. It asks us to examine the impact of the economic decisions we make as individuals, corporations, and a nation on the well-being of all human persons throughout the globe. The bishops call us to recognize the moral content and real consequences of the full range of our economic activities; to discover "in our own place and time what it means to be 'poor in spirit,' and 'the salt of the earth,' and what it means to serve 'the least among us' and to 'hunger and thirst for righteousness' " (Pastoral Message #4).

3   The third, and perhaps most important, purpose of the pastoral is to call us to conversion, to a change of heart and mind, to a recognition of the ways in which our current economic structures and lives fall short both of the Gospel ideal embodied in the love command and of the ideals on which our nation was founded (#14, 294). The bishops sum up the scope and intent of *Economic Justice for All* when they write, "We are called to shape a constituency of conscience, measuring every policy by how it touches the least, the lost and the left-out among us. This letter calls us to conversion and common action, to new forms of stewardship, service and citizenship" (Pastoral Message #27).

Responding to the Pastoral

In order to respond to this call to conversion we need to reflect on the understanding of love, justice, and mutuality which grounds the pastoral and provides the foundation for transforming ourselves and our world. We need also to reflect on experiences such as anxiety, individualism, and psychological numbness which hamper our free and full living out of the vision of the pastoral. Finally, we need to search out ways of overcoming these hindrances in order to live out more fully and effectively the Gospel command of love.

The Gospel Vision: Love, Justice, and Mutuality

The dynamic center of our lives as Christians is located in the free, gracious, and unconditional love of God for us. This love of God for us is expressed and concretized in the realities of creation, covenant, and community, providing the foundation and driving force for our lives. It is God's exuberant, limitless, and enduring love which spills over into the act of creation making all things and making them good. And it is this same love which calls forth a free response from us, which calls us into a covenant of love and a community of commitment and care.

Love

The heart of the Christian tradition is the dual command to love God above all else and to love our neighbor as ourselves. It is a call to respond to God's love by loving in the same way that God has loved us. The love we are called to is the love which St. Augustine called *caritas,* or charity, a rightly ordered love in which the good things of this world are used and appreciated, but never abused. It is a love which recognizes the impossibility of loving God and my neighbor without also loving myself. The love which is *caritas* appreciates the good things of creation and the basic goodness of our human longings, desires, and loves, knowing that it is through these very things that God draws us beyond ourselves transforming our lives.

Justice

Our love, when it truly mirrors God's love, is characterized by freedom, mutuality, and acceptance. It is concretized in love for our neighbor and expressed through justice. For justice is nothing more than the application of love to the concrete circumstances of our daily lives. If love of neighbor is the test and mark of the genuineness of our love for God, justice is the concrete manifestation of love and a condition for love's growth.

The pastoral is a call to love more fully by examining the concrete ways in which our economic decisions, policies, and actions bring about or fail to bring about real justice in our world. It is a reminder that, "explicit reflection on the ethical content of economic choices and policies must become an integral part of the way [we] relate religious belief to the realities of everyday life" (#21).

Mutuality

This grounding vision of love expressed in justice leads the bishops to emphasize the importance of concern for the poor and the marginalized, reminding us that, "The way society responds to the needs of the poor through its public policies is the litmus test of its justice or injustice" (#123).

It is here that we feel the tension between the ideal to which we are called and the real circumstances of our individual and collective lives. For the bringing about of justice in our world will require at times that we forgo some of those goods of creation that we are called to affirm and appreciate, that we temper some of our own longings, desires, and potential so that others may have access to basic human rights and the opportunity to develop their gifts and potential.

Here we come up against both the limits and the paradox of our human situation. If we wish to effect justice we must go beyond justice to love. For love, in every concrete, historical situation, manifests itself in terms of justice; while a true justice always finds itself judged, transcended, and transformed by love.

Jesus as Model

The life and death of Jesus provide the model for the kind of love to which we are called, a love which has at its center a genuine being-for-the other. Jesus' entire life as well as his death was an expression of unswerving commitment to mutual love and justice. The example of Jesus "finally, and most radically . . . calls for an emptying of self, both individually and corporately, that allows the Church to experience the power of God in the midst of poverty and powerlessness" (#52). Our lives must be rooted in that same dynamic love, a love which goes beyond our highest moral aspirations, a love expressed in a genuine love of self combined with a genuine self-giving and self-forgetfulness.

IMPEDIMENTS TO THE VISION

While we hear the Gospel call to love and justice, the call to conversion and repentance, often we find it difficult to respond. We find ourselves holding back, unable to take the first step. Three impediments to enfleshing the vision of the pastoral in our lives seem particularly pervasive in our times: anxiety, individualism, and psychic numbness.

Anxiety

While we live in an age marked by anxiety, the anxiety we experience is not peculiar to our time. It grows out of the very nature of our existence as human beings. We are created free, capable of shaping the future in both creative and destructive ways. We likewise have the capacity to imagine the future we are shaping. This combination of freedom and imagination leads to anxiety. We stand before an open future recognizing the infinite possibilities for creativity and destructiveness, and we grow anxious. Often we respond to the anxiety we experience by inordinately seeking security at the expense of others. We strive to escape our limits and weakness by amassing power, prestige, or material goods.

The expression of anxiety through the inordinate seeking of security pervades our daily lives and our society. We see it in the way in which we close our eyes to realities which are troubling or discomforting. We do not see the hungry or the homeless. We do not see the waste in our own daily lives. And we do not see the connection between the two. Anxiety leads us to accumulate an excess of material goods, allowing our wants to expand into needs. We come to value ourselves and others in terms of what we have rather than in terms of who we are. And we see the inordinate seeking of security at the expense of others most dramatically in the continuing arms race which diverts minds and money to building weapons of destruction rather than to the building of the human community (#23).

Individualism

Our age is marked not only by anxiety, but also by an excessive individualism which pervades our culture and our mentality. Our heroes are autonomous, self-made, and self-sufficient, the cowboy riding off into the sunset. Self-reliance is considered virtuous, dependence questionable. We play to win. We work to stay on top. We learn to look out for number one, quite forgetting the none of us wins unless all of us win. As a result, we find ourselves isolated and alone, without communities of care and commitment, without a company of friends and believers to support and sustain us in our efforts to live the Gospel. This excessive individualism which fosters competitive relationships focused on self-interest, is an outgrowth of our anxiety. It represents a reliance on self which leaves little or no room for reliance on God or others.

Psychic Numbness
The third major impediment to enfleshing the pastoral in our daily lives is the experience of psychic numbness—a protective state in which we withdraw from the pain and suffering around us shielding ourselves from emotional involvement and investment. It emerges in response to the massiveness and complexity of the issues facing us. We feel overwhelmed and powerless in the face of forces beyond our control. We don't know how to feed the hungry or shelter the homeless. We feel powerless to stop the escalating arms race. And so we withdraw into our own homes closing the door behind us, hoping we can build a safe haven from the pain and suffering which surround us. Yet the more alone we find ourselves, the more difficult it becomes to face the anxiety and insecurity within us and the pain and suffering around us.

THE JOURNEY TO THE KINGDOM

The pastoral calls each one of us to conversion, to change our hearts and minds, and to refound our lives on the love which is at the heart of the Gospel message. Conversion is a lifelong, step by step process which begins with accepting ourselves right where we are, with the acknowledging that we are human beings who are weak, fallen, anxious, but who are also accepted, forgiven, loved, and empowered by the love of God. It is this fundamental acceptance of ourselves which opens us to that acceptance of others which is the foundation of love and justice.

The journey of conversion calls us to open our eyes and our minds to see things we have not seen before; to see our own lives as they are, the reality of other lives which are different than ours, and the connections between our lives and those other lives. It involves letting ourselves know the real human beings behind those other lives, looking into their eyes, feeling their pain, hearing their suffering, and allowing our hearts to change.

COMMUNITY

But we cannot take the risk of seeing and hearing anew, of changing our hearts and our minds all by ourselves. ". . . conversion . . . is not undertaken alone. It occurs with the support of the whole believing community, through baptism, common prayer and our daily efforts, large and small, on behalf of justice" (#24). It is this experience of community, of a company of friends and believers who keep faith and heart and hope with us, which makes conversion possible. It is the community which both accepts and challenges us, which invites us to the next step and walks along with us in our struggles, that has the power to transform our lives and our world.

When we experience ourselves as held and challenged by people who love us, believe with us, and believe in us, we find ourselves empowered, able to reach out in concrete ways to neighbor and stranger, able to cooperate with, nourish, and sustain others rather than compete with them, able to envision new and more just ways of restructuring our economic realities at all levels of society.

ENFLESHING THE VISION

With the support of a community of care and commitment we can begin to live out the vision of the pastoral by taking the risk of seeing our world as it is. We can allow ourselves to enter with our imaginations into the realities of poverty, to imagine and feel inside ourselves what it means to be hungry, homeless, uneducated, to be poor and powerless. We can begin to see the real needs of those around us, the way in which our having more than we need leaves others with less than they need, and our inordinate seeking of security helps keep others poor and powerless.

And we can begin to imagine a different world, to see new possibilities for making a difference. For our journey of conversion must above all be rooted in Christian hope, a hope which not only sees what is but also believes in what can be. The restructuring of our lives and our society so that both are expressions of that love to which we are called and by which we are held calls for courage, vision, and imagination. We have to imagine a better world and believe its possibility before we can hope to bring it about.

SYMBOLIC ACTION

The community of believers also enables us to overcome psychic numbness by reminding us that the actions we take make a difference, that by our daily involvement and non-involvement in world affairs we are shaping our world. As our lives become rooted in the Gospel vision of love and justice we come to know that our actions, both large and small, count; that every time we choose less rather than more, every time we curb our desire to accumulate goods at the expense of others, every time we fast in solidarity with the hungry or keep vigil in solidarity with the homeless and oppressed, we change the face of the earth. For every time we do these things we expand our own awareness, we change our own consciousness, we move more fully into the process of conversion.

WIN AS MUCH AS YOU CAN

At the end of these reflections we return to the metaphor with which we began. If we wish to win as much as we can then we must make sure that everyone wins; we must recognize and honor the fundamentally social nature of our lives as human beings. If we wish to turn our world around then we must work together to change our minds and our hearts, to feed the hungry and shelter the homeless. If we wish to transform our world through love, then we must support and challenge one another in our efforts to bring about justice. In emphasizing the importance of the option for the poor the bishops are, in effect, reminding us concretely of what we must do if all of us are to win, for they remind us that ". . . the deprivation and powerlessness of the poor wound the whole community" (#88). If the poor are fed, clothed, housed, educated, and empowered, the lives of each of us will be enriched and the whole human community will benefit. For to the extent that we allow our lives to be formed and transformed by the community of believers into a people who act justly, love tenderly, and walk humbly with our God (Mi 6:8), we will know the deepest longings of our hearts to be satisfied.

FURTHER READINGS

Bellah, Robert N., et al. *Habits of the Heart*. Berkeley: University of California Press, 1985.

Niebuhr, Reinhold. *Justice and Mercy*. Edited by Ursala Niebuhr. New York: Harper and Row, 1974.

Palmer, Parker J. *The Company of Strangers*. New York: Crossroad Publishing Company, 1981.

Tillich, Paul. *The Courage to Be*. New Haven: Yale University Press, 1952.

QUESTIONS

1. What are some of the positive ways in which we can build a security which is rooted in the Gospel into our lives?

2. How do some of the concrete economic choices which we make as individuals and families have an effect on the lives of others?

3. What are some of the specific actions we can take as individuals and families in order to bring a little more love and justice into our world?

4. What steps can we take to help create the communities of care and commitment which will enable us to make a difference?

10

Liturgy and Social Justice

Edward Foley, Capuchin

ANY DISCUSSION WHICH PRESUMES A LINK BETWEEN LITURGY AND social justice suggests, for many, a most unlikely marriage of topics. The publication of the U.S. bishops' pastoral on the economy raises questions which naturally fall within the purview of ethics or moral theology, and would clearly benefit from historical reflections and scriptural insights. Approaching the topic of social justice—or more specifically the economic pastoral—from a liturgical perspective, however, might strike the casual observer as quite far fetched.

This is true, at least in part, because most Roman Catholics think that "liturgy" is a synonym for "Mass." Liturgy thus conceived is fundamentally a rubrical activity relegated to Sunday morning, confined to the sanctuary area, and focused on spiritual rather than material or social matters. Though a common phenomenon, this is nonetheless worship as escape: the obligatory weekly retreat from lived Christianity, which makes no room for the grim realities of poverty or unemployment in its holy precincts. Liturgy so defined seems light years removed from questions of economics or social justice.

This apparent gap between liturgy and the tough issues addressed by the economic pastoral, however, can and must be resolved by moving toward a more encompassing and authentic definition of liturgy. Such will help us to understand that liturgy is not merely a series of rituals to be performed, but a way of living in the world: not fundamentally concerned with vesture or worship aids, but with mission and justice. It is especially in Jesus that this absolute connection between liturgy and life becomes clear, and so his life will be an important focus for our discussion. An introduction to the meaning of liturgy in the life of Jesus, and its continued significance in the early Christian community, will then prepare us to consider how our own rituals are really corporate rehearsals of our mission. Finally, we will consider how the eucharist is a particularly powerful rehearsal of our baptismal call. Hopefully such a progression will not only enable us to understand how a single economic pastoral relates to liturgy, but more essentially how liturgy itself is a central metaphor for the Christian journey.

THE LINK BETWEEN LITURGY AND LIFE

Toward a definition of liturgy: The original meaning of the word liturgy is roughly equivalent to "public service," or "work undertaken on behalf of the people." In ancient Greece, where the term originated, this could have meant producing theater pieces, providing a banquet at a festival, or even exercising one's responsibility to vote. Whatever the mode, however, "liturgy" implied service on behalf of the wider community. When the word was employed in the translation of the Hebrew Bible into Greek, a narrowing of the meaning occurred and "liturgy" primarily designated cultic actions of the priests and levites (e.g., Ex 28:35), though even here a strong ethical undercurrent remains.

From its usage in the Hebrew Scriptures, various forms of this word found their way into the New Testament, where Jesus himself is called *litourgos* or "minister of the sanctuary" (Heb 8:2). The term "liturgy", however, did not exclusively refer to cultic acts in the New Testament, as was primarily true of the Hebrew Scriptures. Instead, it is successively employed to refer to the duties of state officials (Rom 13:6), the collections for Jerusalem (Rom 15:27), the service of an apostolic envoy (Phil 2:25), and even the proclamation of the Gospel (Rom 15:16). It is true that later in the Christian era, the word was again used in a more limited, cultic sense. This, however, can be considered as an unfortunate narrowing of its New Testament meaning.

Liturgy in the life of Jesus: It is precisely in the life of Jesus that the full meaning of the word "liturgy" comes to light. In the course of the Gospels we encounter numerous instances where Jesus prays. He prays in the midst of a gathering of disciples (Jn 17) and in seclusion (Mt 14:23); before a miracle (Jn 11:41f.) and after a miracle (Mk 6:46); at the beginning of his public ministry (Lk 3:21) and at the farewell meal with his disciples (Mt 26:26); at the moment of his transfiguration in glory (Lk 9:29) and in his final agony on the cross (Mt 27:46). Besides the various passages which depict Jesus praying, there are also a number of texts which present Jesus' teaching about prayer. Here we learn that prayer is to be unceasing (Lk 18:1), confident (Mt 18:19), from the heart (Mk 11:23), and always centered on the one Jesus called "Father" (Mt 6:9).

What is most striking about this impressive testimony concerning prayer, however, is neither its frequency nor variety, but rather the absolute integrity between the way Jesus prayed and the way he lived. Jesus centered his prayer on the one he called "Father" because he centered his life on the same. He was able to pray and preach the word, because he lived the word— he was the word. Jesus could challenge others to prayer without ceasing because his own life was a single, ceaseless prayer. Communion with God, personal mission and service to others were not unrelated elements in Jesus' life, but different facets of a single reality.

Our contention that prayer in the life of Jesus was not a retreat from life or mission, but a rehearsal of the same is underscored in Luke's accounts of Jesus' baptism (3:21), his selection of the twelve (6:12), and his teaching of the "Our Father" (11:1). In each of these instances, a moment of mission or instruction is wedded to an experience of prayer. So, too, was the whole of Jesus' mission and teaching one with his prayer.

Jesus' liturgical legacy: This Gospel memory of Jesus as the one who perfectly integrated union with God, personal mission and human service, is echoed in the New Testament instructions on prayer and discipleship for the early church. It is especially Paul who understands prayer as an unceasing Christian experience

(Rom 1:9). This constant commitment to prayer, however, does not exempt anyone from vigorously working for the kingdom (2 Thes 3:6–12). Paul well comprehends the essential link between how one prays and how one lives: thus he rejoices when blessing and service are joined (Rom 15:27), and erupts in anger when some dare to enter into cultic worship while ignoring the needs of others (1 Cor 11:17–32).

It is this fundamental link between liturgy and work for the kingdom, perfectly fused in the example of Jesus and reiterated by Paul, which defines authentic worship and establishes the Christian agenda. It is an agenda which demands an uncompromising union of ethical living and common prayer, and presumes at least the desire for an ethical life as a prerequisite for genuine worship. This Christian ideal is given classic expression in the early moments of the Acts of the Apostles. Here the Lukan summary of the primitive Christian experience inextricably links common life and common worship (Acts 2:42–47). It is this same ideal—once and for all established in Jesus—which continues as the true "liturgical" standard for every age.

The U.S. bishops demonstrated their understanding of this connection between liturgy and life in the message accompanying their economic pastoral, which noted:

> Our faith is not just a weekend obligation, a mystery to be celebrated around the altar on Sunday. It is a pervasive reality to be practiced every day in homes, offices, factories, schools and businesses across our land. We cannot separate what we believe from how we act in the market place and the broader community . . . (#25)

The pastoral itself echoes these insights when it calls for "a deeper awareness of the integral connection between worship and the world of work" (#329). It is only such a perspective which prevents liturgy from degenerating into a rubrical spectacle and preserves it, instead, as the enacted belief of the church.

LITURGY AS A REHEARSAL OF JUSTICE

Now that we have introduced a more encompassing definition of Christian liturgy, and illustrated the intrinsic connection between worship and Christian living—especially as revealed in the life of Jesus—it is necessary to explain how liturgy can be considered a "rehearsal" of the Christian mission. More specifically, we will attempt to illustrate how Christian liturgy is both an expression of and impetus for justice, and is in itself a just act. Such a discussion will prepare us to further consider how the eucharist is a special rehearsal of our mission in justice.

Liturgy as font and summit: The first document of the Second Vatican Council, the Constitution on the Sacred Liturgy, states that "the liturgy is the summit toward which the activity of the Church is directed; at the same time it is the fountain from which all her power flows" (#10). Worship, thus conceived, exists at the very center of the Christian experience, which the Constitution reaffirms when it continues, ". . . the goal of apostolic works is that all . . . should come together to praise God in the midst of His Church" (#10). This is liturgy as "summit" and summation of the Christian mission. Consequently, all that we do—all ecclesial energy expended in the proclamation of the Gospel—finds its purpose and fulfillment in the gathering of the baptized to give thanks and praise.

Besides this "expressive power," however, the Constitution also notes that the liturgy has what might be considered a "creative power." Herein we recognize that worship not only announces what has been accomplished, but also proclaims what is yet to be achieved: is not only a summation but an introduction. Thus our common prayer not only announces salvation in Christ, but simultaneously engages us in the ongoing work of salvation; it not only reveals the church to be holy but directs us to new ways of holiness. Accordingly, the Constitution admits worship's power to inspire the faithful "to become of one heart in love . . . (and) prays that they may grasp by deed what they hold by creed" (#10). This is liturgy as font and source of the Christian life.

These two facets of Christian worship—one expressive, the other creative—lead us to the heart of worship's power. They also begin to reveal why we can call Christian worship a rehearsal of our mission in Christ. Liturgy, rightly understood and lived, is not an empty statement about a distant God or ideal human relationships but is rather a symbolic activity: what the bishops in Music in Catholic Worship call "vehicles of communication and instruments of faith" (#7). The act of worship integrated with human life, therefore, creates the reality it signifies. Consequently, we are not only informed of our incorporation into the Body of Christ, but through Christian initiation we are in fact incorporated; we are not only assured that Christ is made present through the consecrated bread and wine, but are ourselves transformed into his body and blood.

This is what it means to call liturgy a "rehearsal" of the Christian life. Rehearsal, in this sense, is not a meaningless repetition of the same action in order to perfect it. Rather, it is a continual reentry and further appropriation of a rich and inexhaustible reality. Rehearsal so imagined is neither artificial nor preparatory: it is rather ritual engagement with the truth. To experience again, for example, a performance of Arthur Miller's classic "Death of a Salesman" is thus a rehearsal: a fresh confrontation with the questions of meaning and success which gnaw at our national conscience. To yearly commemorate the birthday of Martin Luther King is to personally and collectively rehearse again his challenge and his dreams. Analogously is our entry into the Christian mysteries a rehearsal of the call offered to us in faith, and simultaneously a foreshadowing of what our response is to be.

It is in this sense that liturgy can further be understood as a rehearsal of justice. Justice is traditionally defined as giving to others what is their due. Christian worship is, in turn, giving God what is God's due *dignum et justum est*—for this is *right* and *just*. Liturgy is consequently a paradigmatic just act. Besides directing our attention to the Holy One, however, worship further links praise with human care and service: encouraging us to support each other in faith, to be reconciled, and to share peace. Therefore, baptism, marriage, and all other liturgical acts rehearse just relationships by recognizing the dignity of others in Christ. Liturgy is not, therefore, an escape from the social ills which confront humankind—just as it is not a way of holding God at bay. Instead, worship catapults us into the social arena where the kingdom is to be proclaimed *and* served.

Eucharist and the Economy: Our journey from a broad definition of liturgy to the acknowledgment of worship as a just act finally leads us to a consideration of Christian eucharist. The economic pastoral itself recognizes that there is an intrinsic link between eucharist and the world food problem today:

> The problem of hunger has a special significance for those who read the Scriptures and profess the Christian faith. From the Lord's command to feed the hungry, to the eucharist we celebrate as the Bread of Life, the fabric of our faith demands that we be creatively engaged in sharing the food that sustains life. There is no more basic human need. (#282)

If Christian liturgy is a rehearsal of who we are to be as followers of Jesus, then the example of Jesus who fed the hungry, nourished the outcast, and was recognized in the breaking of the bread compels us to attend to the cries of the hungry.

More than calling for charity to the hungry, however, the celebration of eucharist also seems to offer a critical reflection on the economy itself. As Enrique Dussel has demonstrated, eucharist presupposes that people have bread and wine at their disposal, both of which are "works of human hands." Eucharist, therefore, presumes the existence of an economy. More than this, however, eucharist also presumes that people have some basic control over the economy and are free to give their produce back to God. Specifically, the eucharistic gesture of "offering" assume that we have bread to give and wine to return.

What happens, however, when the produce is not free to offer or when there is not enough food to satisfy basic human needs? Is it possible to celebrate eucharist when some do not even control the fruit of their own labor, or even have the opportunity for work? When the promise of the earth becomes perverted, and workers can no longer feed their families, much less offer from their earnings to God, then the potential for authentic Christian eucharist is greatly diminished.

Dussel would go even further, and suggest that the example of Jesus demands not only the ability to give produce back to God, but also the freedom to share with the poor, to whom the kingdom is promised. Eucharist at its core, therefore, rehearses a just economic system in which gifts can be offered to God and human hungers be satisfied. This is the presumption of the church's worship, ritually enacted in the offering of produce and praise, and the sharing of communion. The eucharist thus rehearses not only the messianic banquet of the next life, but an authentic Christian banquet in this life. To the extent that such is not encouraged or does not exist, can one question our capacity to fully celebrate Christian eucharist.

Conclusion

In his book *On Liturgical Theology*, Benedictine liturgist Aidan Kavanagh notes that ". . . the liturgy of a church is nothing other than that's church's faith in motion on certain definite and crucial levels" (p. 8). Worship in this perspective is not the fulfillment of a Sunday morning obligation, an elaborate artistic endeavor, or even a moment of cosmic appeasement, but "faith in motion." The U.S. bishops have acknowledged that the economic arena is one of the chief places where we live out this faith and liturgy is where such faith is rehearsed. It is only by maintaining this connection between the altar and the marketplace that our faith can be put into motion and, in the example of Jesus, authentic worship rendered "in spirit and truth" (Jn 4:23).

FURTHER READINGS

Dussel, Enrique. "The Bread of the Eucharistic Celebration as a Sign of Justice in the Community." In *Can We Always Celebrate the Eucharist?*, edited by Mary Collins and David Power. *Concilium* 152. New York: Seabury Press, 1982. pp. 56–65.

Hellwig, Monika. *The Eucharist and the Hunger of the World*. New York: Paulist Press, 1976.

McKenna, John. "Liturgy: Toward Liberation or Oppression." *Worship* 56 (1982) 291–308.

Searle, Mark, ed. *Liturgy and Social Justice*. Collegeville: The Liturgical Press, 1980.

Seasoltz, R. Kevin. "Justice and the Eucharist." *Worship* 58 (1984) 502–525.

QUESTIONS

1. What are the connections you perceive between liturgy and social justice in your own community?

2. Are there concrete ways in which the social outreach programs of your local church can be integrated with your common prayer?

3. Does the liturgy nourish your personal commitment to justice, or could it?

4. Is it possible to think of your public worship as either a ritual of inclusion or one of exclusion?

11

The Pastoral's Challenge to Religious Education: The Living Word

Jeanette M. Lucinio, S.P.

MOST AMERICANS WOULD NOT THINK OF THE ECONOMIC CHOICES they make as religious choices. Yet that is the message of *Economic Justice for All: Catholic Social Teaching and the U.S. Economy.* The U.S. bishops challenge us to see our faith and spirituality embodied in our purchases, our work, our investments, and our economic policies. We cannot keep faith and economic decisions in separate compartments of our lives.

DUAL CHALLENGE FOR ALL WHO TEACH

As teachers, parents, campus ministers, and religious educators at all levels, we are doubly challenged by this letter. First, *we* are invited to respond to its prophetic call to a change of heart. Then we are asked to assist our students in processing what they already feel and sense about the issues listed in the pastoral. As teachers and parents we are called to enable our young people to grow in their understanding of the Scriptures and the church's teachings. This requires great sensitivity and care on our part. We must listen to our children. What are their questions? What are their fears and their concerns? How can we help them experience the love and fidelity of God and the biblical call of economic justice for all?

Conversion and repentance we may think apply to others but not to us. However, Christians are continually called to conversion. Jesus himself began his public ministry with a call to repentance. To *re-pent* means *to think about again.* The pastoral letter, with its theme of justice for all, rests firmly on scriptural foundations and calls for conversion:

> We have presented the biblical vision of humanity and the church's moral and religious tradition as a framework for asking the deeper questions about the meaning of economic life and for actively responding to them. But words are not enough. The Christian perspective on the meaning of economic life must transform the lives of individuals, families, in fact, our whole culture. The Gospel confers on each Christian the vocation to love God and neighbor in ways that bear fruit in the life of society. That vocation consists above all in a change of heart: a conversion expressed in concrete deeds of justice and service. (#327)

The biblical references made to creation, covenent, community, and the call to discipleship are very familiar to us. We have read them or heard them countless times throughout our lives. We know them well. Or do we? Could it be that we are being called by God in our time to "repent" of our familiarity of the Scriptures? Could it be that we need to take a fresh look and be courageous enough to discern our cultural temptations? *"From the patristic period to the present, the church has affirmed that the misuse of the world's resources or appropriation of them by a minority of the world's population betrays the gift of creation since 'whatever belongs to God belongs to all' "* (#34).

A METHOD OF THEOLOGICAL REFLECTION

The call to a change of heart is first addressed to the "leading learner," the one who teaches. With Scripture in one hand and the pastoral in the other, we begin our study. This process can be carried out alone or with colleagues. It is based on a method of theological reflection suggested by James and Evelyn Whitehead in their book *Method in Ministry* (Seabury, 1980).

1) Read and internalize the message of the pastoral. Prayer-

fully give time to it and allow yourself to be challenged by its call.

2) Ask yourself: (a) What is the focus of each section? Do you agree with what is written? With what do you disagree? (b) What parts of the pastoral are disturbing to you? Are there ways you can resolve this? (c) Is your position in balance with the biblical message? (d) How can you introduce concepts from the pastoral to your children or students? Will they feel comfortable doing this?

CLASSROOM AND ENVIRONMENT ASSESSMENT

Take a look around your classroom, homeroom, Newman Center or home. Ask yourself:

1) What images are displayed? Do they reinforce stereotypes that alter a young person's understanding of human dignity? What kinds of books, posters, games, and other learning resources are readily available? What messages do they communicate? Competition? Cooperation?

2) As "leading learner" how does your behavior affect the environment? Are young people experiencing the love of God for them through your respect of and care for them as individuals? Do you model justice? What kinds of rules do you have? What kind of discipline?

3) Are the young people learning to be interdependent? Assess your students' play, their physical education, their sports teams. What is their attitude about winning? How do they treat losers? Can they cope with failure?

4) What are some new concepts you can introduce to them that will foster cooperation and interdependence?

Educating at Various Levels

There are no hard and fast ways of preparing to teach the concepts of the pastoral. Those who educate must be sensitive to the developmental levels of their students. They must watch for the "teachable moments" as times when students are most ready to learn. Religious values are learned most effectively when they are integrated into the students' perception rather than superimposed from the outside.

One way of integrating concepts from the pastoral into lesson presentations already being taught is called *infusion*. The models presented here are based on those devised by the Justice and Peace Education Council of New York.

ELEMENTARY GRADES

Concept: "The Biblical Vision of Creation."
Lesson: "God's World Is Good" (Primary)
Aim of Lesson: To help the children: *know* that God made the world; *appreciate* God's creation; *give thanks* for creation.
Concept from the Pastoral: Creation is a gift. We are to be faithful stewards in caring for the earth.
Suggested Activity: Take the children outdoors on a creation hunt. Ask them to find something wonderful that God has given us. Instruct them to choose something small that will fit in their hands.
Activity Related to the Pastoral: Direct children to decorate a paper lunch bag as gift-wrap. Tell them that they make their treasures even more special by giving them to friends. Invite them to place all the bags in a large box. Let each child select a new bag.

Concept: "Interdependence." "We have to move from our devotion to independence, through an understanding of interdependence, to a commitment to human solidarity" (#361). Students of every age can be assisted in discovering how their actions and choices affect the quality of life of others.
Lesson: "Participation" (Intermediate)
Aim of Lesson: To help the students recall that participation means giving as well as receiving, and to realize that when we participate in the life of God's people, Jesus is with us.
Concept from the Pastoral: Interdependence.
Suggested Activity: Make up short plays about participating and not participating.
Activity Related to the Pastoral: Assign students to be ambassadors from several countries about which they have studied in geography. Ask them to gift-wrap a special commodity from their particular nation which they would like to share with the others who lack it and who would benefit from it. Discuss what would happen if they kept their gift just for themselves.

JUNIOR HIGH, SENIOR HIGH, YOUNG ADULTS

Concept: "Jesus Calls Us to Follow Him"
Lesson: "The Image of Christ"
Aim of the Lesson: We come to see who Jesus is by reading the Scriptures. They help us to understand that Jesus has an important role in (a) shaping the young person's response to the challenge of living a Christ-like life; (b) discovering through prayerful reflection on the Scriptures the call to conversion; (c) enabling the student to choose the image of the *servant* Christ to guide them in developing an attitude of caring and concern for others.
Concept from the Pastoral: Union with Christ trancends all divisions of sex, race and social status (Gal 3:28) and means that we can never be indifferent to those who suffer material and spiritual deprivation or who are victims of injustice.
Suggested Activity: Write the words "Independent," "Dependent," and "Interdependent" on poster or chalkboard. Have the group list ideas that come to mind under each word. Point out the differences between real strength and rugged individualism, weak dependency and the strength of admitting one's need of others, and helping the needy and admitting one's needfulness.
Activity Related to the Pastoral: Discuss the meaning of "responsibility" as "the ability to respond." What is holding back a nation so rich in resources from responding to the needs of others?

The above examples are offered to spark creative energies and to point out ways in which one can infuse concepts from the pastoral into what is already being taught. For more information about the infusion method, write: Justice and Peace Education Council, c/o Secretary, 20 Washington Square, New York, New York 10011.

FAMILY CATECHESIS

Parents are reminded in the midst of the celebration of the rite of infant baptism that they above all others are the primary religious educators of their children. Most parents are apt to feel inhibited when asked to discuss faith with their children. Yet how families live together at home each day is far more important to a child's faith development and moral formation than all the theology and religious instruction in the world.

In one way or another, all of us have been influenced by the "American Dream" or the "American Way of Life." It has been held out to us as the path leading the unlimited possibilities for happiness and success if only we work and compete hard enough. The bishops' pastoral calls for a rediscovery of the meaning of life and new degrees of happiness and fulfillment. Families are challenged to reconsider their lives and their values which are so influential in determining the atmosphere in which their young members are growing up.

Many of the suggestions already cited in this chapter can be easily carried out with in family circle. It is recommended again that parents take an environmental assessment of the home. What images are displayed? What books and magazines are possessed? What games do our children play? What values do we put on the latest fashion or brand of consumer goods? How do family members see us reverencing the earth and conserving its resources?

Reflect on your family's favorite TV programs, news coverage, commercial ads and popular songs. What do they say about success, wealth, happiness and real human hungers and needs?

Invite family members to keep track of a week's activities. Ask yourselves: (a) To what do you devote most of your time and energy? To what do you give your best time and energy? (b) How do you spend your money? What do you buy? (c) What do your economic decisions reveal about your family values?

Through personal reflection consider your family's need for reconciliation and healing. Remember the times you failed to forgive, to listen to one another or reacted with indifference. Take this opportunity to notice loneliness or the hunger for love and attention within the family before gazing outward to notice the exploited, the poor in our neighborhoods. Talk to your children about the need to "re-pent," "to think again" about life's values and commitments. At the heart of all repentance is the call to mend relationships. Believe that healing is possible and take the first steps toward renewing the family bond.

Parish Reflection

The parish pastoral staff could be invited to do a reflection on how the parish allocation of funds reflects gospel values. It could also reflect on whether the parish forms partnerships that are mutually beneficial to the parish and the local business community. Perhaps the parish could sponsor some basic sessions on how the economy works. Invite an economist to address the group. Parishes might celebrate Labor Day and the Feast of St. Joseph the Worker with a lively catechesis on labor. This could be accompanied with a celebration of the crafts produced by the men and women of the parish community.

REFLECTION ON LIFE

In a fast-moving, radically changing world, a revolution in values is affecting society, particularly youth and young adults. Because the economic pastoral challenges these values, it risks being ignored and even rejected by American Catholics. In his book *Christian Religious Education* (Harper and Row, 1980) Thomas H. Groome reminds us that many recent religious education theorists have proposed a *praxis* way that is experiential/relational and active/critically reflective on lived experience as it is informed by the biblical message. *Praxis* means "reflection on life." It means learning by doing and learning from what we are doing. The author attempts to deepen the critical reflection on experience and holds present experience in a dialectical and critical correlation with the Story and Vision (The Kingdom of God). What does the Story say to our present praxis? What does present praxis do to and ask of the Story?

> The Kingdom is already among us whenever and wherever God's will is done . . . But given the reality of sin in ourselves and in our world, there are ways in which the Kingdom of God is not yet. Thus the Vision of the Kingdom enables us to discern the limitations of our present praxis that are not of the Kingdom, and calls us to a Christian praxis that will be more creative of the Kingdom and more faithful to God's invitation . . . For while the Kingdom is a measure of and a promise to our present, that Vision

is also an open future being shaped by present praxis, and our knowing of it is possible only as we shape it. (p. 197)

The following are a few suggestions of topics for such critical reflection. Participants express their own views, listen to the views of others and then place their own reflections on life (praxis) in dialogue with the Christian Story. In this process they are challenged to come to a response in living faith as called for by the pastoral.

The bishops remind us that:

The pattern of Christian life as presented in the Gospel of Luke has special relevance today. In her Magnificat, Mary rejoices in a God who scatters the proud, brings down the mighty and raises up the poor and lowly (Lk 1:51–53). The first public utterance of Jesus is, "The Spirit of the Lord is upon me because he anointed me to preach good news to the poor" (Lk 4:18; Is 61:1–2). Jesus adds to the blessing on the poor a warning: "Woe to you who are rich, for you have received your consolation" (Lk 6:24). He warns his followers against greed and the reliance on abundant possessions and underscores this by the parable of the man whose life is snatched away at that very moment he tries to secure his wealth (Lk 12:13–21). In Luke alone Jesus tells the parable of the rich man who does not see the poor and suffering Lazarus at his gate (Lk 16:19–31). When the rich man finally "sees" Lazarus, it is from the place of torment and the opportunity for conversion has passed. (#48)

1) Ask the students: What are the parables for our time? Where are the conversion moments that make us the "light of the world? How do we contribute to or break the cycle of poverty in which so many find themselves caught because of the economic situation today? How do we treat the *Lazaruses* of our society (the homeless, the welfare mother, etc.)?

2) Invite the students to do a budget (a theological reflection). Have them write the budget within which they have lived this past month, listing what they have spent on clothing, movies, recordings, recreation, food, etc. Ask them to trace the impact of their choices on others.

3) Send the students to experience the unemployment office. Have them interview persons on fixed incomes.

4) Mature students, Newman Center groups or adults could be challenged to adopt an elderly person. Students could be introduced to the St. Vincent de Paul Society in their parishes in order to accompany the members as they serve the poor.

Upon their return ask them: What is the economic profile of the neighborhood? How has it changed? Look beyond the socio-economic level. What is the basis of the economic life of the community? Do people in the community work in the community? What services do the people get for the taxes they pay? Is everyone equally served? What about the neighboring grographic area?

5) Ask students to price commodities in the stores of their neighborhood. Then compare these prices with those in a neighboring area. Help the students become aware of the interlocking of nationwide discount chains. Help the students discover who the parent companies are.

6) Help students understand the wage range of the textile workers in Hong Kong or other places in the Far East or Latin America. Trace the number of jobs that have been lost in the United States because some companies have moved their manufacturing out of the country.

7) Trace the ways the media covers the economy. Familiarize the students with the basic vocabulary of economics: Dow Jones, GNP, etc. Study the World Bank and how it affects the economy of other nations.

8) Invite students to investigate volunteer opportunities for the Campaign for Human Development or other outreach development programs.

Conclusion

The concluding paragraph of the pastoral (already quoted) returns once again to the theme of personal conversion. It may well be that this document and its companion pastoral on peace are the prophetic calls of our day. As teachers at all levels we stand in the tradition of proclaiming the Word.

Christians today are called by God to carry on this tradition through active love of neighbor, a love that responds to the special challenges of this moment in human history. The world is wounded by sin and injustice, in need of conversion and of the transformation that comes when persons enter more deeply into the mystery of the death and Resurrection of Christ. The concerns of the pastoral letter are not at all peripheral to the central mystery at the heart of the Church. They are integral to the proclamation of the Gospel and part of the vocation of every Christian today. (#60)

But unless the *Word is living in us,* it remains a dead letter on a flat page.

FURTHER READINGS

Hug, S.J., James E. *Scripture Sharing on the Bishops' Economic Pastoral.* Kansas City: Leaven Press, 1985. (A series of reflections and discussions based on the Lenten Sunday Scripture readings.)

The Bible Today 21:3 (May 1983). (A special issue exploring the biblical background of the peace pastoral.)

Whitehead, James D. and Evelyn Eaton Whitehead. *Method in Ministry.* Minneapolis: Winston-Seabury Press, 1980. (Valuable for its methodology for theological reflection.)

Yu, Mary and Sr. Cathy Campbell, S.P., eds. *The Challenge of Peace: God's Promise and Our Response: Implementing the Pastoral.* A joint project of the Office of Justice and the Office for Catholic Education of the Archdiocese of Chicago in cooperation with the Illinois Catholic Conference, 1983. (An excellent guide for teaching the peace pastoral. Many of its ideas can be adapted to the economic pastoral.)

12

Communicating the Pastoral

Fred Hang, C.S.S.R.

COMMUNICATING ECONOMIC MATTERS IN A PASTORAL SETTING HAS never been a simple task. Whether teaching, preaching or presenting a talk to a parish organization, a communicator is well advised to expect a wide range of responses when economic issues are involved. For example, there is a story told of a country preacher who was speaking very pointedly one day. The preacher said, "Now, sisters and brothers, let the church walk." The assembly answered aloud, "Amen, let it walk." The preacher then said, "Let the church run." Again the assembly responded, "Amen, preacher, let it run." Spurred on by their enthusiasm the preacher continued, "Now my brothers and sisters, let the church fly." "Amen, amen!" yelled the assembly, "Let it fly, let it fly!" Then, after a long, deep breath, the preacher said, "Now it's going to take money to let the church fly." "Let it walk," groaned the assembly, "Let it walk."

Giving the Pastoral Wings

In the pastoral letter on the economy the U.S. bishops are calling the church to the urgent task of working toward economic justice for all. They are, in effect, urging all of us to not only walk, but to run and fly with the mission of communicating the Christian vision for economic life. Concluding the pastoral, the bishops acknowledge that the letter is "but a beginning of a long process of education, discussion and action . . . its contents must be brought to all members of the church and society" (#359). Communicating the contents of this pastoral in a variety of pastoral settings (preaching, teaching, retreats, seminars, etc.) is the challenge before us now. But realistically, how do we give such a massive document "wings"? How do we go about putting this challenge into action?

I suspect that after some initial enthusiasm on the part of many already overworked church communicators, the response to the pastoral may soon turn to, "Let it walk," or at best, "Let it run its course." It is not hard to imagine a good number secretly arguing, "I haven't even digested the peace pastoral yet, and now I'm being asked to communicate the newest one!"

First, let us wrestle with some of the difficulties and objections that may arise when attempting to communicate from the pastoral. Then we will examine two rather common questions which audiences and assemblies bring to many communication contexts, and discover how the pastoral may serve as a rich resource for addressing these questions. Finally, we will ponder the beginnings of a model from which to communicate the pastoral, a model which emerges in part from the method in which the pastoral itself was composed.

Wrestling with the Difficulties

One of the first difficulties a communicator may face when teaching or preaching from the pastoral is a subtle but very real resistance. This resistance finds expression in the widespread tendency in our society to separate the sacred and the secular. "Keep politics out of the pulpit." "Don't mix economics with the Scriptures." These and similar sentiments illustrate the importance of being tuned into your audience's experiences and frame of reference. I may be convinced that economic justice and the Scriptures are integrally connected in living the Christian life. And certainly the bishops go to great length to demonstrate that "the concerns of this pastoral are not at all peripheral to the central mystery at the heart of the church. They are integral to the proclamation of the gospel and part of the vocation of every Christian" (#60). Communicating this, however, and actually leading people into making the moral and spiritual connections between the Scriptures and the economy which lead to action, demands a sensitivity to the audience's point of view. In an excellent publication on preaching (*Fulfilled in Your Hearing*, USCC, 1982), a point is brought home which I believe applies to all communicators: "Preachers may indeed preach on what they think are the real issues, but if they are not in touch with what the people think are the real issues, they will very likely be misunderstood or not heard at all."

Related to the issue of being aware of the audience's frame of reference is the matter of the credibility of the one who communicates. How much credibility does an audience or assembly perceive a cleric or religious to have, for example, when presenting a talk or preaching on economic issues? There are some who would argue that these would be among the least credible since many are removed by their special lifestyle from some of the harsher economic realities of daily life (e.g., unemployment, poverty, welfare, strikes, etc.). Anyone who attempts to communicate effectively from this pastoral is well advised to ponder their own credibility. In the process we will do well to study the riches of the past and present social teaching of the church and to be immersed in the word of God in prayer and reflection. We need also to continually challenge ourselves to verify information, validate assumptions, and above all, *listen* unceasingly to the voices and stories of those who experience the economy from vantage points other than our own.

A final area of concern related to speaker credibility is the bishops call to self-examination on the part of the church herself. "While the church is bound to give witness to justice, she recognizes that anyone who ventures to speak to people about justice must first be just in their eyes. Hence we must undertake an examination of the modes of acting and of the possessions and lifestyle found within the church herself" (#347). This self-examination must begin with the individual communicator.

Let's wrestle with one more difficulty that those who would communicate the pastoral may face: the temptation to avoid it altogether because of its sheer size and the complexity of the issues it raises. "What can I possibly say that is really going to make a difference anyway? Whatever I communicate will not even begin to put a dent in unemployment or world hunger, or end poverty or job discrimination." No doubt the temptation to this way of thinking arises for many of us at times, especially when results of our previous efforts are hard to see and feedback is even scarcer. Still, we are wise to resist this temptation. "We may hide behind the complexity of the issues or dismiss the significance of our personal contribution, but in fact each one has a role to play, because each of us makes economic decisions" (#329).

Christian communicators have the vocation to speak a word of hope and challenge, of vision and direction. This calls for avoiding oversimplification and naive optimism, as well as not ignoring the harder issues or coloring them with cynicism. Anyone attempting to communicate the truths laid out in the pastoral will do well to keep these closing remarks from chapter 2 in mind: "The Church's experience through history and in nations throughout the world today has made it wary of ideologies that claim to have the final answer to humanity's problems. Christian hope has a much stronger foundation that such ideologies, for it rests on the knowledge that God is at work in the world, 'preparing a new dwelling place and a new earth where justice will abide.' This hope stimulates and strengthens Christian efforts to create a more just economic order despite difficulties and setbacks" (#125–126).

Not having immediate answers or foreseeable results to the complex issues the pastoral raises need not discourage communicators. Rather, we should allow the tension between the promise and fulfillment, which is a constant theme in the Scriptures, illumine the issues and shape the words of our messages.

So What . . . Such as?

A common complaint today toward much of the communication that takes place within the church is the failure to bring the message of the Scriptures and our tradition to the daily, lived experience of those who hear it. This complaint can best be summarized in two questions which members of our audiences and assemblies often carry with them. They are rarely stated in exactly the same words and are seldom spoken aloud. But a sensitive communicator is always aware of their existence when planning a message or speaking. Stated as simply as possible, these questions are: so what? . . . and such as?

So what difference does following Christ and living the Gospel make in my life and the life of my neighbor? It is one thing to offer pious platitudes and generalized religious sentiments, but in what concrete ways am I to live the Scriptures here and now in the 1980s? Such as? For example? It is here, with these quests for relevancy and concreteness, that the pastoral offers the communicator a rich resource. Of particular interest in addressing these questions are chapters two and three.

Chapter two, "The Christian Vision of Economic Life," offers a solid, if selective biblical basis for discerning issues of economic justice. A wide variety of texts are suggested as springboards for the development of a number of timely and crucial themes to communicate in classroom, pulpit or other contexts. These include: the dignity of the human person, the call to creative engagement with God's handiwork; the biblical bias for the an-awim in matters of justice. The cardinal points of Israel's faith are outlined here (creation, covenant, and community) as well as the New Testament themes of the reign of God and disciple-ship. A prayerful reflection on these themes and texts, combined with self-examen and a listening ear to the experiences of others, offer the communicator more than ample resources for address-ing the "so what" questions of the audience/assembly. To par-aphrase a section from this chapter, the communicator "is summoned to be an instrument in assisting people to *experience* the liberating power of God in their lives, so that they may respond with freedom and dignity. (Both the communicator and the assembled) are called to an emptying of self, which will allow the church to experience the power of God in the *concrete realities* of poverty and powerlessness of our times" (#52).

In chapter 3, "Selected Economic Policy Issues," four very concrete subjects are examined which offer the communicator the beginnings of many specific examples from which to address the "such as" questions the listeners often bring. These four are: employment, poverty, food and agriculture, and the U.S. role in the global economy. Time spent reflecting on these related issues which touch the speaker's life, will offer many specifics from which to "*encourage* reforms which hold out hope for trans-forming our economic arrangements . . . and challenge practices and institutions (and attitudes!) which impede or carry us farther away from realizing the Christian moral vision" (#126).

To underscore the importance of dealing with the "so what,

such as" questions of your listeners, consider this old tale. A centipede suffering from arthritis went to the wise owl for advice. The owl thought for long time and then replied, "Centipede, you have one hundred legs swollen with arthritis. My advice is that you change yourself into a stork. With only two legs you would be cutting your pain by 98 percent. Then by using your wings to stay off your legs you wouldn't have any trouble at all." The centipede was delighted with the suggestion and asked the wise owl just how he could change into a stork. The owl replied, "Oh, my heavens, I wouldn't know about the details, I offer only the general policy."

The communicator who presents only the general policies and themes of the pastoral runs the risk of never seeing the heart of its message take flight. Without concrete stories and experiences drawn from reflection, the word, and the lives of those who would communicate it, the pastoral remains 'general policy.'

Concluding Thoughts

There will be as many ways and approaches of communicating the pastoral as there are communicators. A few final suggestions, however, are offered by way of conclusion. These serve only as a starting point, a "model" if you will. The communicator's own creativity, and faith experience must shape the rest of the task.

Begin with the conviction that the realization of a Christian vision of economic justice is a communal task (cf. #123). Before composing the first sentence of your talk or sermon or lesson plan, spend time in dialogue with a mixture of members from the community you will address. I am suggesting here that the process of preparing to communicate the contents of the pastoral should reflect the process of its composition. Throughout the various drafts the bishops respected the maturity and co-responsibility of the people in asking for feedback, experiences, and insights. We can do no less.

Second, a very special sensitivity must be given to the point of view of the poor and the powerless. When praying and reflecting on the specific topic you hope to communicate from the pastoral, do so with the compassionate vision the pastoral itself calls for. "A compassionate vision is demanded . . . which enables the church to see things from the side of the poor and powerless; to assess lifestyle, policies and institutions in terms of their impact on the poor" (#52). This vision best respects the Scriptures themselves which are written from the point of view of the weak and powerless. An outstanding resource for helping the communicator develop and refine such a vision is the work, *Liberation Preaching: The Pulpit and the Oppressed,* by Gonzalez and Gonzalez.

Finally, in preparing to communicate the pastoral do not overlook the imagination. The bishops employed this when, in chapter 4, they envision "a new American experiment." We who communicate the pastoral now will do well to also employ a hopeful imagination in envisioning concrete Christian responses to social and economic realities never envisioned in times past (cf. #61).

Now my fellow communicators, to really allow the message of the pastoral to fly will call for our continued dialogue, prayer, self-examen and responsible and imaginative reflection . . . "Let it fly . . . let it fly."

FURTHER READINGS

Bishops' Committee on Priestly Life and Ministry. *Fulfilled in Your Hearing: The Homily in the Sunday Assembly.* Washington, D.C.: United States Catholic Conference, 1982.

Foley, O.P., Nadine, ed. *Preaching and the Non-Ordained: An Interdisciplinary Study.* Collegeville: The Liturgical Press, 1983.

Gonzales, Justo L. and Catherine G. *Liberation Preaching: The Pulpit and the Oppressed.* Nashville: Abingdon Press, 1980.

QUESTIONS

1. How would I describe the *audience* or *assembly* to whom I will most likely speak? Do I think they will most likely respond to my communication on the pastoral? What is the best way of verifying this before I speak?

2. As I read and ponder the pastoral myself, where do the questions "So what?" and "Such as?" arise for me?

3. What gives me *credibility* to speak about the pastoral? Is this likely to be perceived by my audience/assembly? How can I become an even more credible communicator?